Minefields
of the Heart

Related Titles from Potomac Books, Inc.

*"War Stories": False Atrocity Tales, Swift Boaters, and Winter
Soldiers—What Really Happened in Vietnam*
—Gary Kulik

Through Veterans' Eyes: The Iraq and Afghanistan Experience
—Larry Minear

*Help! I'm a Military Spouse—I Get a Life Too! How to Craft
a Life for You as You Move with the Military, Second Edition*
—Kathie Hightower and Holly Scherer

Claim Denied! How to Appeal a VA Denial of Benefits
—John D. Roche

The Veteran's PTSD Handbook: How to File and Collect on a Claim
—John D. Roche

The Veteran's Survival Guide: How to File and Collect on VA Claims
—John D. Roche

Minefields of the Heart

A MOTHER'S STORIES OF A SON AT WAR

SUE DIAZ

Foreword by Jim Frederick

Potomac Books, Inc.
Washington, D.C.

First Paperback Edition 2013
Copyright © 2010 by Sue Diaz

Published in the United States by Potomac Books, Inc. All rights reserved. No part of this book may be reproduced in any manner whatsoever without written permission from the publisher, except in the case of brief quotations embodied in critical articles and reviews.

Parts of this book originally appeared in earlier versions in the *Christian Science Monitor*, the *San Diego Union-Tribune*, *Newsweek*, *Child Magazine*, and *Family Circle*. Adapted and reprinted by permission.

"A New Assignment, Another Trip Home" originally appeared as a "My Turn" essay in the February 21, 2005, issue of *Newsweek*.

"War" originally appeared as "As My Son Goes Off to War" in the *San Diego Union-Tribune*, March 20, 2003.

"Once More to the Lake" originally appeared as "The Last Word: A Mother's Thoughts on a Son at War" in the *San Diego Union-Tribune*, August 4, 2005.

"A Christmas Apart" and "Attack at Yusufiyah" originally appeared in the *San Diego Union-Tribune*, on December 25, 2005, and June 23, 2006, respectively.

Library of Congress Cataloging-in-Publication Data
Diaz, Sue.
 Minefields of the heart : a mother's stories of a son at war / Sue Diaz. — 1st ed.
   p. cm.
 Includes bibliographical references.
 ISBN 978-1-61234-653-3 (paperback)
 ISBN 978-1-59797-563-6 (electronic)
 1. Iraq War, 2003—Social aspects—United States. 2. Soldiers—Family relationships—United States. 3. Diaz, Roman. 4. Diaz, Sue. 5. Mothers and sons—United States—Biography. I. Title.
 DS79.767.S63D43 2010
 956.7044'31—dc22

                                        2010019563

Printed in the United States of America on acid-free paper that meets the American National Standards Institute Z39-48 Standard.

Potomac Books
22841 Quicksilver Drive
Dulles, Virginia 20166

First Edition

10 9 8 7 6 5 4 3 2 1

For all who have served
and
those who love them

Contents

Part Two:
AT HOME AND BETWEEN DEPLOYMENTS

Part Three:
THE HELL OF WAR

Part Four:
THE JOURNEY HOME BEGINS

Acknowledgments

Special thanks to my mentor and friend, Michael Grant; to the manuscript's earliest readers: Sharon Bray, Mary Curran-Downey, Susan Denton-Dere, Virgil Irwin, Janet McDermott, Linda O'Quinn, Josie Rodriguez, Candace Toft, and Kathy Zakoski; to Clara Germani and the editors at *Christian Science Monitor*; to my editor at Potomac Books, Hilary Claggett; to the intrepid veterans in the writing workshops at the San Diego Vet Center and Veterans Village of San Diego; and to my family: Roman Sr., Anne, Erick, Jesy, and young Roman, who continues to teach us the meaning of courage.

Foreword

On March 15, 2010, I received an e-mail from someone named Sue Diaz. I did not know Sue Diaz, but during that spring it was not uncommon for me to get mail from strangers. About a month earlier, I had published a book called *Black Hearts: One Platoon's Descent into Madness in Iraq's Triangle of Death*. As the subtitle indicates, it was a rather blunt look at a particularly brutal subject: the 2005–2006 deployment of one company of soldiers—Bravo Company, First Battalion, 502nd Infantry Regiment, 101st Airborne Division—to perhaps Iraq's most dangerous region at arguably its most dangerous time. The Triangle of Death, which was about twenty miles south of Baghdad, served up daily doses of carnage to the 135 men of Bravo Company. Bravo's First Platoon suffered a particularly high death toll and a breakdown in leadership that led to an epidemic of poor discipline and unsoldierly conduct. Such bad behavior would, among some men of the platoon, spiral and intensify, culminating in an unspeakable atrocity. Four First Platoon soldiers would go on to commit one of the worst crimes of the war: the rape and murder of a fourteen-year-old Iraqi girl and the murder of her parents and her six-year-old sister. Despite the undeniably unsavory subject matter, I tried throughout my research and writing to maintain what Norman Mailer called a "severe compassion" for everyone in the unit and all the Iraqis that they encountered. Without excusing such a brutal crime, I tried to understand how the unthinkable actually happens.

In the weeks following publication, the book received several favorable reviews and was embraced by a wide range of civilian and military readers (including many members of Bravo and the other companies of First Battalion). I started receiving e-mails from readers who said they were touched by the book. I was always flattered and gratified when I received feedback, but especially when it came from the men of Bravo, their wives, or other family members. Those were the readers who meant the most to me.

Sue Diaz was, I thought, one such correspondent. The subject line of her e-mail, after all, said, "Message from mother of soldier in Black Hearts." Before clicking the message open, I had already recognized her last name. She must be, I thought, the mother of Sgt. Roman Diaz, whom I had interviewed during my research and who makes a few small but unambiguously positive appearances in my book—brief glimpses of combat heroism, short but clear-eyed quotes about the untenable nature of the whole company's situation—creating fleeting but strong impressions that if the platoon had been filled with more guys like Roman Diaz, things might not have ended so badly.

But the content of Diaz's message was quite different from those of most of the moms who had written me. "You and I share a connection," she wrote. What she meant by that, she went on to explain, was that we were both journalists (I for *Time*; she for the *Christian Science Monitor*), and we had both written books about the Black Heart Brigade. Mine was already out, obviously, but hers had yet to be published. Would I read it, she wanted to know?

I did. And I am glad I did. I sat down to read it on a Sunday afternoon, and I did not put it down until I had finished it. Not quite a memoir, not quite a collection of essays, *Minefields of the Heart* is exactly like the boxes filled with newspaper clippings, photos, report cards, childhood drawings and other milestones of a life—boxes filled with memories—that form one of the earliest and most enduring metaphors of the book. However, this is not to suggest that it is not finely written. *Minefields of the Heart* is very finely written, which is why I kept turning page after page after page. Because a mother's love is so overpowering, so singular in its focus, I had half-feared that this book would be a morass of melodrama. But Diaz is a disciplined and careful writer, and this, ultimately, is where the power of her book comes from. She is spare where most writers would be mawkish, she is understated where most writers would be sentimental, and she understands that life, death, war, grief, gratitude, and the loss of innocence—hers and her son's—need no baroque writerly adornments. The truly great and terrible stuff of life is most dramatic when told as simply and plainly as possible. Over the course of her book, due to Diaz's finely tuned "severe compassion," the reader comes to know not just Roman, but the whole Diaz family and how they all aged and matured both during and after Roman's two harrowing deployments.

Sue Diaz was right. We do share a connection. In some ways, our books are oddly complementary. My book tells the story of a year-long deployment of an entire infantry company. Eighty-three soldiers are mentioned by name. And, quite consciously, I located almost all of the action of *Black Hearts*, geographically and psychologically, in Iraq. I pay almost no attention to the soldiers' families or home lives—or even their thoughts of home. In framing my book that way, I aimed to emphasize just how far away the very idea of home is, just how alien a war zone is, just how distant the notions of kin and kindness and love and familiarity are when men are engaged in combat for prolonged periods of time. My book purposely shut out the home front.

Minefields of the Heart, on the other hand, is all told from the home front. It is all about what goes on in a mother's and a family's life when a family member goes to war. I was fascinated—and touched, frequently to the point of tears—to see the life story of Roman Diaz (whom I had only known as Sergeant Diaz, soldier and veteran) unfold in this carefully curated collection of his mother's memories. By focusing on the intensely personal and specific—the silly name Roman gave his turtle, the way he surprised his family by joining the Army at all (let alone the infantry), and his quiet selflessness (such as when he insisted his family charge a nice dinner out on him even as he was deep in a war zone)—Diaz has managed to make her family's plight both unique and universal. Her work is a window into the ordeal that every service member's loved ones endure with every deployment, and for that she has done us a great service by making their sacrifices palpable.

—Jim Frederick, author of *Black Hearts:*
One Platoon's Descent into Madness in Iraq's Triangle of Death

Introduction

"It is only those who have neither fired a shot nor heard the shrieks and groans of the wounded who cry aloud for blood, more vengeance, more desolation. War is hell."

— *Gen. William Tecumseh Sherman, U.S. Army, 1861–1865*

BOXES

Home on leave in San Diego for the first time since his second deployment in Iraq had ended, my twenty-three-year-old son, in jeans and a T-shirt, sat at the desk in the bedroom at the end of the hall. There he clicked away on his new laptop, a Mac he'd purchased at a Nashville mall just a few days after his unit with the 101st Airborne Division returned to the States in the fall of 2006.

"Hey, Mom. Come here," Roman said, catching a glimpse of me in the hallway. "Want to see some of my pictures from Iraq?"

He hadn't talked much about the war those first days he was home. And I'd avoided asking a lot of questions. That seemed the best thing to do, given what we here at home had learned from news stories about the last months of his time with the 101st's 502nd Infantry Regiment, a unit known since World War II as the "Black Heart Brigade."

"Pictures?" I said. "Sure."

Coming to stand beside him, I cupped my hand on his shoulder and fixed my eyes on the screen.

Click. A group of Army buddies leaning against a dusty Humvee. Click. Rows of recovered mortar shells. Click. Camels trotting down a rutted road. Click. A helicopter silhouetted against a blood-red sky. Click. Iraqi children waving. Click. Shattered buildings. Click. The blackened frame of a burned-out car. Click. Click. Click.

Intermittently my gaze slipped from the screen to a framed collage on the wall just above the desk. Photos from another time. Roman riding his first two-wheeler. Swimming in the kiddie pool on the patio. Rollerblading. Cradling a pet iguana. Playing computer games. Posing at Knott's Berry Farm.

The slideshow clicked on. I interrupted it now and then to ask, "Where was that?" or "Is that your squad?" A few times Roman pointed out some of the guys in the group photos, saying, almost wistfully, as if he were surprised to see them again, "There's Chaca!" or "Tuck!" Nicknames of soldiers he'd lived with and fought beside. Young men who, I knew from those stories on the evening news that summer, would never grow old.

For the most part, the photos came and went with little commentary. That is, until a haunting close-up of Roman stared out from the screen.

"The day this picture was taken," he began, then paused. I waited. My hand moved from his shoulder to the side of his face, and with the back of it I stroked his cheek, sliding downward from the small indentations, shrapnel's etchings, near his eye.

He started again. "The day this picture was taken . . . was the worst day of my life."

"Oh, Roman," I whispered as that sank in. "That week in June?"

He nodded, then quickly clicked to another photo. And another. And another. Photos that mirrored a country at war, not—like the one I'd just seen—a soul.

～

This is a story about boxes. Mine contains news clippings about that day in Iraq—what led up to it and what came after. It's a brown leather box where I've also stored notebooks, journal entries, essays published with my byline, photos, letters, and printouts of online conversations. A scrapbox of sorts, filled with bits-and-pieces connected mostly to Roman and to the past few years.

My son has his box, too. It is the one that soldiers returning from war carry within themselves, the box that holds everything a combat vet has seen and felt and heard and done in the line of duty.

The reality of impending death—one's own or someone else's—is a fact of life in war. The taking of human life—a bedrock taboo of peacetime society—becomes a necessity in the context of combat. Military training turns "Thou Shalt Not Kill" into "Kill or Be Killed." For the young soldier, war is a world with a whole new set of rules.

In his book, *Out of the Night*, William P. Mahedy, coauthor of the design for the national Vet Center program, examines the morality of war and writes: "Even though killing enemy soldiers amounts to legitimate self-defense in a combat zone, something about it is very wrong. The harsh reality of combat may leave individuals no choice but to kill in a given situation, but the GI survivor knows somehow that both he and his dead enemy have been sucked into unspeakable evil."[1]

As the daughter of a World War II veteran, I know it's not uncommon for vets to want to keep the lid on their memories. Opening up can take some time. Years, for some. Decades, for others. Many never do.

But it's important to try. In his groundbreaking book, *Home from the War*, Robert Jay Lifton says, "confrontation (with the war experience) involves acknowledging something one dimly knew but kept oneself from consciously recognizing." Confrontation, Lifton continues, leads to discovery. "That discovery is related to an image of death (such as 'People can die,' 'Death exists for me'). . . . The other side of discovery, an inseparable part of it, is a glimmering of renewed life, of the possibilities of integrity, connection, and movement."[2]

For the past year I've been leading writing workshops for war veterans at the San Diego Vet Center through a grant from a local foundation. It is work that brings together two lifelong passions of mine: writing and teaching. The personal connection I feel to those who have served also plays an undeniable role in my Vet Center work.

Each Wednesday afternoon, a cadre of veterans from wars as far back as Vietnam and as recent as Iraq, gathers around a table in a small room at the Center to write and share their stories. War stories that in some cases, they've never shared before. What they've written in their spiral notebooks on those

Wednesdays has given me a glimpse into the boxes they have carried with them from places like Danang and Fallujah, Saigon and Sadr City.

Through the stories these veterans have been brave enough to write, they have been my teachers. In listening I've learned—among other things—that in the unrelenting pressures of a combat zone, the new rules of war sometimes get bent, blurred, or in the worst situations, horribly twisted. A truth acknowledged by the slow nods and knowing looks that often pass between the guys after one of them has read. "Been there," they say, without saying anything.

The words "Open at Your Own Risk" are stamped all over their boxes, because what's inside can be scary as hell. There, the wounded still writhe in pain, the eyes of the dead stare up at skies impossibly blue, people—the good and the bad—lay in pieces, and the bomb that killed a best buddy keeps on exploding.

Every vet knows the contents of his own box all too well, perhaps even to the point where it's lost its power to frighten him. What veterans do fear, I think, is the judgment of those who haven't walked the patrols they've walked, manned the checkpoints they've manned, or had to make the wrenching split-second decisions that have been theirs to make: Friend or foe? Stop or go? Hey! Why's that kid standing in the middle of the road in front of our convoy?! Fuck! Is that a grenade in the hand of the woman who keeps walking—Stop!!!!—toward us?!

According to psychologist Peter Marin, one sure thing combat vets carry home with them from war is the knowledge that "the world is real; the suffering of others is real; one's actions can sometimes irrevocably determine the destiny of others; the mistakes one makes are often transmuted directly into others' pain; there is sometimes no way to undo that pain—the dead remain dead, the maimed are forever maimed, and there is no way to deny one's responsibility or culpability, for those mistakes are written, forever and as if in fire, in others' flesh."[3]

~

That autumn afternoon standing next to Roman and his Mac, the image of his haunted face still burning its way into my brain, I didn't know all that his box held. I wasn't sure I wanted to. I could only guess at the memories he brought home with him, could only imagine the burden that was his box.

Roman Diaz, age 6. Photo by Sue Diaz.

My soul has housed its share of boxes, too. In one of them: memories of the child who loved all creatures great and small; the quiet, curious boy who would one day—inexplicably, it seemed to me—choose to become a soldier in the U.S. Infantry.

I held on tightly to that box throughout the time Roman was in the war, a war I never believed in. Maybe my stubborn grip reflected denial, pure and simple, of the new reality I found hard to accept. Or perhaps holding on to those memories reflected a mother's belief that beneath the Kevlar vest her son now wore, and inches away from the strap of his automatic weapon, thumped a heart as good and as gentle as she remembered. And nothing could or would ever change that. Not even war. Could it?

Into a far corner I kicked another psychic box of mine. The one with the word "Anger" scrawled in large, uneven letters across the side of it. Its flaps were folded in on each other, and most of the time it stayed closed. But every now and then, something came along to jar that container, loosening those flaps enough for some of what was inside to finally spill out.

The biggest box by far was marked "Worry." Anyone who has ever loved someone living in a combat zone will tell you there's no getting around that one. And a good part of the reason is the fact that it is love that forms the base of that box. If we didn't love, we wouldn't worry. It's as simple—and as complicated—as that.

Worry was still with me as I stood in the bedroom at the end of the hall thinking about the photo I'd just seen, the one taken on what Roman described as the worst day of his life. He didn't say more about it than that. I didn't know if he ever would. Perhaps there are no words for what those eyes in the photo begged to unsee.

Part One:
THE ROAD TO WAR

LIFTING THE LID

Outside the light rain that fell earlier today drips off the leaves of the eucalyptus onto the slats of the patio cover, puddling near the base of the sliding glass door. Rainy days here are rare, and usually call for a change in plans. But this weekend's weather turns out to be perfect for a project I've put off too long: cleaning out my side of the closet in the master bedroom.

Standing before the closet's open door, I debate what to deal with first. A brown leather box, nearly hidden by a second-tier line of blouses and blazers, catches my eye. With its white stitching and strap-like handles, it looks more important than most boxes relegated to the back of a closet. And it is. I wriggle it off a low shelf and carry it over to the bed.

Photo by Sue Diaz.

Let it be. Leave it alone, a voice inside my head says. *You've got other things to sort through this afternoon. Do you really want to revisit the stuff that's in this box? Roman's been back from Iraq for a year and a half now. The war's over for him, isn't it? Let it stay that way—for you, too.*

I sit down beside the box and run my hand across its smooth surface. My eyes travel over to the digital clock near my husband's side of the bed. A new minute flips into place. A few more follow.

Taking a deep breath, I lift the lid.

Inside, a loose assortment of papers, and a fair share of things I wrote—some from the several magazines and newspapers I freelance for, others written simply to record events or to try to make sense of them, at least on paper. Most of what's here is related to Roman's time in the service. A few stories from farther back than that have found their way in. Here's a column about Roman's first day of school I wrote for a local parenting magazine many Septembers ago. So long ago it seems "Once upon a time" would be an apt beginning.

I remember writing it, and read it now for the snapshot it gives of Roman's complex character, and for the clues it offers into a choice he would make fourteen summers later.

~

Early September 1988. With a group of other parents, I am lingering on the schoolyard blacktop, heart in throat, as my youngest child and his new classmates line up for the very first time behind a paper sign that reads: Kindergarten—A.M. When the 8 o'clock bell rings, Roman's public school education will officially begin. Soon he'll be learning the rudiments of phonics, new number concepts, and the importance of sharing—not to mention the second verse of "Itsy-Bitsy Spider" and where to find the bathroom pass. My little boy, going out into the larger world. A Milestone Moment.

I sigh, bite my bottom lip, blink back a few silly-me tears. Gazing off into the distance, I square my shoulders and silently vow—for both our sakes—to be strong.

Suddenly, I feel a small tug on my arm. It's Roman. He's slipped out of line and come over to me. Curling his forefinger, he indicates there is something he needs to tell me, something important, but it's a secret. What? I wonder, bending toward him. Does the little guy, here on the brink of The Great Unknown, need some last minute reassurance? A quick kiss? A kind word to carry with him to the crafts table?

He cups his dimpled hand over my ear, takes a deep breath. After a moment's pause, I hear him whisper, "You can go now, Mom."

The bell rings. Faster than you can say, "Good morning, boys and girls," Roman's back in line. Tossing a crooked grin in my direction, he bustles with the others toward Room B-3. If I want a long last look, I'll have to settle for the back of his head.

The morning passes with the loose routines of a writing mom who works at home: dishes, laundry, time on the computer. It is close to noon. I've come back this time with my mom, Roman's grandmother, visiting from Arizona. The two of us are sitting on a low concrete bench near the kindergarten room, waiting to greet him after his first day.

"I don't see him, do you?" my mother says with a cluck of concern as her eyes scan the line of five-year-olds wriggling its way back from the playground.

"Well, he's gotta be there somewhere," I say, "That's his teacher, Mrs. Bennett, near the front."

We look again, our eyes bumping across a line that's advancing with all the precision of a drunken centipede. Arriving at the classroom, Mrs. Bennett smiles benevolently and waits for the last of the kids to disappear inside. Then her arm reaches behind and closes the door.

My mother and I look at each other.

"He wasn't with them, was he?" I say.

"I don't think so, dear."

I get up and peek through the narrow window of the door. I see the children clustered on the carpet, sitting cross-legged, looking up at their teacher. Clearly she is saying Very Important Things. It is also clear to me that my son isn't in the room to hear them.

"I'll be right back," I turn to tell my mom.

On a hunch, I head over to the playground. In the distance, on the far side of the slide, I catch a glimpse of a small figure in a red polo shirt sitting in the sand. His head is bent down. I see only the top of it, but I'd know that wispy, white-blond hair anywhere. Roman is hard at play, oblivious to anything but the grains of sand streaming through his fingers.

"Roman, what are you doing!?"

He looks up. Smiles.

"Oh, hi, Mom."

His attitude is ultra-casual, la-dee-da.

"Recess is over, Roman. The teacher called the rest of your class inside. Why on earth are you still here?"

"Well," he says, patting a growing mound of sand, "No one called me."

Some kids cling. Others, right from the start, can't seem to crawl away fast enough. They are who they are, these children of ours. Sometimes early on, life grants us an illuminating glimpse of those traits of theirs that will perplex and challenge us for years to come. On that first day of kindergarten, I was struck by my son's self-possession, his singular focus, the strength of his independent spirit. Good things, all. At the same time, too, I couldn't help but worry, that in marching to the beat of a different drummer, he would also risk missing a good part of the parade.

That was Roman, demonstrating early on a sense of self. That's clear to me now. And with my mind's eye, I see the-soldier-he-would-become stride across that sandy playground and, grinning, bend to high-five the-boy-he-used-to-be. In retrospect, Roman's desire for independence at age eighteen should have come as no surprise.

A few years after he started school I watched him riding his two-wheeler at the end of the cul-de-sac—popping wheelies, flying off the curb, making skid marks—and wrote:

I have to make a conscious effort not to be overprotective. And that's not always easy, especially since my sense of impending danger seems to be keener than most. When other parents see a skateboard, I imagine stitches. When others hear the words "class field trip," I envision a lost third-grader leaning over the crocodile exhibit looking for his class. Other parents seem capable of finishing sentences, even pizza, in the midst of a birthday party at Chuck E. Cheese's. I'm momentarily rendered speechless when one of my kids disappears into the sea of plastic balls for more than seven seconds.

There's a tug of war that goes on in my soul as my children get older. On the one hand, there's the parental urge to protect. Like a squirt of sunblock, I want to keep them safe from life's ultraviolet rays—from scraped elbows and hurt feelings, from reckless drivers, lightning storms, and second-hand smoke. I

*want to shield them from a world that's not always kind and sometimes down-
right dangerous.*

*But there's another part of me that knows this isn't possible. There's the
grown-up realist who knows too well that triple dip ice cream cones can topple
and melt, birthday balloons can pop, and those happy bare feet at the beach can
become stubbed toes in the asphalt parking lot. It's true, I think, that the sources
of some of our most exquisite joys contain within them a rattling seed packet
of potential pain. That's just the way it is. The two are interconnected, for better
or worse. To taste one, we have to risk the other.*

My son's younger mother, who seems to know everything—and nothing
at all—continues:

*And this is a lesson my children—all children—have a right to learn, in
spite of our timely "Watch out's" and very sensible "Be careful's." I guess that's
why, as parents, we take off the training wheels from our children's bikes, and
why we sign their permission slips for adventuresome outings, and why we
wave, a little slowly, as they skip around the corner.*

Or march off to war.

ROMAN'S CHOICE

In autumn of 2000, at the start of his senior year, Roman, headstrong as
ever, decided he didn't want to go the college route, at least not right after
high school. After graduation he'd work instead, he informed his dad and
me, at the small start-up where he'd been employed as a Web designer, part-
time, since the summer.

Pleased with the work he had been doing for them, the powers-that-be
there had told Roman that if he wanted, he could have a full-time job with
them come June—with a good salary, benefits, even stock options. The kind of
job parents tell their kids higher education will lead to.

For Roman, Web design wasn't work; it was fun. "I can't believe they're
actually paying me to do this!" he'd told his dad and me many times that year
after another afternoon on the job.

He and his dad, Roman Sr., a software engineer, shared a love of technology. When Roman was fourteen, he built his first computer, an IBM clone. It

started out as a joint father-son project, but—true to form—Roman insisted on doing as much of it as he could on his own.

"Well, it's a good way for him to learn," my husband said, resigning himself, reluctantly, to the role of Tech Support and Transportation Source.

As fate would have it, the start-up company Roman was working for folded shortly after he graduated; the air just beginning to leak out of the dot-com bubble. As for Roman's Plan B, there was none. A four-year university? Too late for that in the fall. Community college? Not interested. A full-time minimum wage job? No thanks.

He'd look for another Web job, he said, not here in San Diego, but in Long Beach, where Jonny, his best friend since their Little League days, had been accepted at the state university there. Freshman dorms that year were overcrowded, and Jonny had to find an apartment near campus. He invited our son to be his roommate.

Roman decided to take him up on the offer.

As the day of his departure from home got closer, I asked if he needed help with anything, thinking he might want to draw on my expertise in the Nitty Gritty Little Stuff of Life: what to look for in a toaster or a steam iron, for instance, or how to choose a coffee filter, a ripe cantaloupe, or a long-distance phone plan.

"Don't worry, Mom," he said. "Everything's under control."

"Really? Do the two of you have a can opener? A frying pan?" I couldn't help myself.

Silence. A level look. Then the words, sighed more than said, "Jonny and I worked out who's bringing what. Some of the stuff that's on my list I'm going to get at Target. Relax, Mom. OK? I can do this."

And he wanted to, too. Needed to, it seemed.

He took with him the essentials: his computer and desk, futon, clothes, his pet snake, a rosy boa named Max, in a plastic sweater box with holes punched through the taped-on top. Easier to transport than the glass aquarium Max used to live in.

On a Saturday in August, he loaded all that and a few boxes more in what used to be the family minivan, his now, a seven-year-old Nissan Quest with two new Michelins and more than 124,000 miles on it, and set out for the one-hundred-mile trip up I-5 to Long Beach.

"I'm not so sure about this," I confided to my husband the day our son left.

"I know what you mean," he said, "but let's look at it this way: At the very least, it'll be a learning experience for him."

And it was. Real life became Roman's classroom. But he found that particular course harder than he'd expected. After 9/11, jobs were scarce for self-taught Webmasters in baggy jeans. As the year went on, he made ends meet—barely—with odd jobs. Loading trucks. Stocking shelves.

"Have you thought anymore about college? We'd help with that, you know," we said to him on more than one occasion when he came home for a weekend visit.

But he stayed as determined as ever to make it on his own. And at the end of his friend's school year in Long Beach, Roman decided to join forces with Uncle Sam.

"I'll have a job. A paycheck. Health benefits. Money for college when I get out. I'll get to see the world, too," he explained. "Plus the structure and the discipline will probably be good for me. And besides," he murmured, "I think I'm ready to be part of something larger than myself."

～

His lease up, his enlistment papers signed, Roman lived at home again for several weeks before leaving for basic training in Fort Benning, Georgia.

It was a strange time. A time of adjustments and redefinition.

"So, where are you going?" I'd ask, slipping back into full Mom Mode when I'd notice him putting on a jacket around the time I was thinking about getting into my pajamas.

"Out," he'd bristle, car keys jingling.

～

At the breakfast table one morning, we were talking about his decision to join the Army. He was scheduled to meet later that day with an Army rep to choose the training and the job that would be his for the next four years.

Through the steam of the coffee rising from the mug he gave me for Mother's Day, my eyes met his. I wouldn't call his expression that day "defiant." His was more the look of a cocky eighteen-year-old with every expectation of living not just to a ripe old age, but, quite possibly, forever.

Because of his high scores on the preliminary test the Army gives all its recruits, Roman's options in the military were many: Computer Programmer. Translator. Multimedia Illustrator. Topography Analyst. Radiology Specialist. Technical Engineer. To name a few.

"I know what I'm going to pick," he said.

"You do? I said. "What's that?"

He shifted a bit in his chair. Looked down for an instant, then up.

"The infantry."

"What!?!"

"The infantry."

"You're kidding!!!"

"No, Mom. I'm not."

"We're not talking paintball here, Roman."

"I know that. But I want to do something physical for a change. You know, challenging. Outdoors. I don't want a desk job. And you know what? The infantry offers the best bonus. Ten thousand dollars!"

"There's a reason for that! Don't you see?" I sputtered.

It was my father's eyes I was seeing then. Dad had been in the infantry in World War II. When my sisters and I were growing up, we'd sometimes ask him about the war. Then the smiling Daddy we knew would suddenly turn somber. His eyes would move from our open faces to something in the distance only he could see.

Once when I was about eleven, I stumbled upon a shoebox in a bottom drawer of an old dresser in a corner of the basement. Curious, I pulled it out and lifted the lid. Inside, a couple stacks of black-and-white photos. Images from my father's war. The war of a foot soldier who, with his comrades from the Army's 7th Corps, had landed on the beaches of Normandy, battled through to Paris, and near the very end of the war encountered, as liberators, what remained of one of Hitler's death camps. That afternoon in the basement, I knew that the photos I was staring at weren't meant for my young eyes. In truth, they weren't meant for anyone's.

～

"My mind's made up," Roman said.

I tried to change it. Wasn't above pleading.

"Please, Roman. Don't make that choice. Don't. *Please.*"

"Why not?"

"You . . . you could get killed!"

I pressed on, searching for as many different ways to say "Don't do this" and "Please" as I could think of, my voice getting higher with every variation.

He sat there, arms folded, hearing me out, but not really listening. With a sigh of exasperation and a tone meant to be reassuring, he finally said, "Come on now, Mom. I've made my decision. It'll be fine. You'll see. It will."

He believed it would be. I didn't. And not only that, this choice of his seemed to go against everything I *did* believe.

I scrambled for another approach to dissuade him. This was too important not to pull out all the stops. I seized on the issue of the bonus, money as a motivator, and remembered a credit union Certificate of Deposit that was earning interest for me on the same sum that Uncle Sam was dangling in front of this new recruit. It had been part of an inheritance from my Aunt Rosie, my dad's sister.

"OK. Tell you what. I have some money I've been saving, a CD worth $10,000. It's yours, if you'll change your mind. Think of it as a bonus for NOT choosing the infantry."

Roman responded with an emphatic shake of his head. Gift or bribe, our much-loved boy, raised by his dad and me to think for himself, to be his own man, would have none of it.

SOLDIER FROM SUBURBIA

The rain has started up again, a strange accompaniment to the stack of stories I'm settling in to read, many of which are set in a desert seven thousand miles from this neighborhood's green lawns. A world away, in more ways than one.

Roman gave me a glimpse into his new life in the military with this conversation near the end of that summer.

~

"No, not like that, Mom. *Like this.*"

I was standing in the family room, and he was teaching me how to salute. I noted how the tips of his fingers lightly touched near his eyebrow. How his hand, wrist, and forearm formed a nice straight line that angled in sharply at his elbow. With his arm lifted like that, I couldn't help but also notice how the waistband of his boxers billowed above the belt loops of his hip-hugging jeans.

I tried again.

"Better," he nodded.

A booklet he'd brought home a few days earlier, compliments of the local Army recruiter, lay open on the coffee table. In it were things every new recruit needs to know, including whom to salute, and how.

As a new recruit, my son had much to learn. And I feared, so did I.

~

Mornings I'd unfold the newspaper and debate whether or not to read the news from the Middle East. Tensions in that region were building. Before then, I'd routinely read news of conflicts in that area and other parts of the world, but that was when the word "troops" was just another word in the headlines.

Now that word had a face, and that face belonged to someone I met for the first time nearly nineteen years earlier in a hospital delivery room. I had looked into my newborn son's eyes then and thought about all that life might hold for him.

Bombs in Baghdad were not on that list.

~

The day before he was scheduled to leave for Basic, I was sitting on the couch, sorting through the mail. Taking a break from packing up stuff in his room, Roman shuffled over, plopped down beside me. Without any sort of preamble, he laid his head on my shoulder. He hadn't willingly done that kind of thing since, I don't know, third grade. I slipped an arm around him, pressed my lips against his bristly hair. Without a word, we sat like that, he and I, as the afternoon shadows of a late summer day grew longer.

~

The next day our family's private D-Day arrived. Roman strode down the hall, his backpack slung over one shoulder. He put it down to say good-bye. At the front door, he and his dad hugged in that self-conscious, men-who-know-each-other-well hug. Then it was my turn. I wrapped my arms around his waist, my tears mottling the front of the T-shirt he just ironed.

"Love you," I blubbered.

"Me, too, Mom," he whispered.

He turned and picked up his backpack. Roman Sr. and I followed him and our daughter Anne, home for the summer from Stanford, out to the car at the curb. Our two kids, born 27 months apart, had always been close. Anne wanted to be the one to drive her brother to his assigned pick-up point that evening.

Roman opened the door on the passenger side, slid into the front bucket seat. Just before he closed the door, he looked over at his dad and me, standing together in the front yard where he used to play hide-and-seek, and my eyes met his.

Suddenly, I found myself lifting my hand, wrist, and forearm to form a nice straight line that angled in sharply at my elbow, making sure the tips of the fingers of my right hand lightly touched near my eyebrow.

With a crooked smile, Roman returned my salute. Then fastening his seat belt and facing straight ahead, my soon-to-be-a-soldier son looked down a road that would lead to a future none of us in that post-9/11 world could be sure of anymore.

BASIC TRAINING, FORT BENNING, GEORGIA

FIRST LETTER HOME, SEPTEMBER 2002

Mom & Dad,

I'm finally in Basic, took long enough though. Nothing in the Army happens very fast. We spent a week processing in the 30th AG [Adjutant General] reception battalion, doing things like getting shots, dog tags, battle dress uniform, PT's [physical fitness tests], etc. etc. It was very boring. I did manage to contract a wicked case of the flu. I'm very sick with a very sore throat. Not the best thing for sounding off . . . but I'll live. Basic isn't as bad as people say. If you don't screw around you get left alone. The atmosphere is very "military." "Duh!" While I write this I can hear mortar fire. There is nothing civilian around. (It's all been taken away while we train.) When we march we sound off with, "Trained to kill! Kill we will!" There are a few other chants, but this one is the cleanest. The food is decent. We get to eat three times a day, but I can't wait for leave so I can get some Buffalo wings or pizza or anything good. I'd do anything for some "Wing 'n' Things" right now. Or coffee. We don't get much sleep. That's about all that is new with me. You can send pictures and letters, but nothing else.

I love and miss you,

Roman

P.S. If it's not too late, tell Dad not to reformat the hard drive I left on my old computer. I had NOT backed up one of the logical drives on it, and I would lose a ton of work. Thanks.

～

Roman's training continued for sixteen weeks: ten weeks of BCT (Basic Combat Training) and six weeks of Advanced Individual Training.

SEPTEMBER 16

I'm still sick, but not as bad. I really miss civilian food. I miss you guys, too. I have the vacation picture of all four of us hung in my wall locker. Good news. I might be able to come home for Xmas. Emphasis on might. I've been hearing that we're going to war with Iraq and if we do I might end up doing that after Basic. Either way, think positive.

～

UNDATED (THIRD WEEK OF TRAINING)

Hey, old folks! How are ya? I'm doing good. I'm barely sick now, although I'm now very sore. Things in Basic have picked up. We've done road marches, gone through the gas chamber, been issued our weapons, and tomorrow we have GFT (Ground Fighting Tactics). Oh, we also went through the obstacle course. Today was the first day of our third week of training. . . .The weather hasn't been great. "If it ain't rainin', we ain't trainin'!" I do miss my computer though. I miss instant access to information on the world around us. We don't even get information on things going on in the Army. I hear we're going to war. . . . Is this true?"

～

OCTOBER 7

We're still training hard . . . my platoon is the best platoon in the company (out of only 3 platoons). My battle buddy gets on my nerves though.

He's nice enough, but he does very poorly in a professional environment. He's slow as hell, so he's always late to formation and stuff. He doesn't try to learn the things we need to learn (like chain of command, the Infantryman's Creed, etc.). I'm not sure how to motivate him.

~

A FEW WEEKS LATER

Last week was a blast. We had Monday off. All we did was watch movies in the barracks. Wednesday we went to the "Soldier Show," a morale booster type thing the Army puts on, kind of like a mini Del Mar Fair. We even got to eat ice cream and pizza! The show itself was soldiers (non-infantry) from other bases singing different popular songs. All in all, it was a pretty good time. This week, however, has been quite a contrast. Monday we qualified for BRM (Basic Rifle Marksmanship). My platoon had the most first-time qualifying people, so of course we took that event too. My platoon has won every event we enter. The next day, we packed our rucks and marched eight miles to a new range to familiarize ourselves with the new weapons sighting system that the Army has. When we road march, we carry our weapons in our hands and 50-lb. rucks on our backs. We walk at the pace of a slow run (we arrived at the range before breakfast). Anyway, we stayed in the field for four days. During the day we were shooting with CCO's (Close Combat Optics) and at night we did night fire exercises with the PAQ-4, an invisible laser sight that is only visible with special night vision goggles. With all that shooting, we didn't sleep much. Every morning we marched a few more miles to a new range. It was a long four days.

LAST LETTER BEFORE HIS UPCOMING GRADUATION FROM AIT (ADVANCED INDIVIDUAL TRAINING)

Thanks for all the recent letters. We're in the AIT phase now and moving at high speed. I haven't had much time to write letters. . . .What's new in the world? I heard Saddam agreed to our conditions or something. So it doesn't look like we'll be going to war. At the same time, last week while I was on a pass, we saw a convoy driving to the airport. I guess Kelley Hill (Fort Benning's infantry unit) is being deployed. Right now troops are all over the place. I really have no clue what's going on. So fill me in.

~

Roman graduated with his group from AIT on December 18, 2002. And he would get to come home that Christmas.

INFANTRYMAN'S CREED

I dig a little deeper in the box through the loose news clippings and airmail envelopes and pull out a printout of "The Infantryman's Creed," a tattered relic from Roman's time in basic training. I remember him telling his dad and me how he and his fellow recruits had been required to memorize these words and be able to recite the Creed on command. More than just a drill sergeant's whim, that exercise seems to me to have been a way to impress upon the young trainees the proud history they would soon be part of. It's a statement of belief—in the trust a country places in its warriors, and in the warriors' commitment, not only to the fight, but also to that faith.

Knowing what I now know about what would happen three summers later in the dust and desolation of a place called Yusufiyah, the words of the Creed mean both more and less than when I first read them.

I am the Infantry.
I am my country's strength in war;
her deterrent in peace.
I am the heart of the fight . . .
wherever, whenever.
I carry America's faith and honor
against her enemies.
I am the Queen of Battle.

I am what my country expects me to be . . .
the best trained soldier in the world.
In the race for victory
I am swift, determined, and courageous,
armed with a fierce will to win.

Never will I betray my country's trust.

always I fight on . . .
through the foe,
to the objective,
to triumph over all,
If necessary, I will fight to my death.

By my steadfast courage,
I have won 200 years of freedom.
I yield not to weakness,
to hunger,
to cowardice,
to fatigue,
to superior odds,
for I am mentally tough, physically strong,
and morally straight.

I forsake not . . .
my country,
my mission,
my comrades,
my sacred duty.

I am relentless.
I am always there,
now and forever.
I Am The Infantry!
Follow me.

TO BASIC TRAINING AND BEYOND—WITH SPONGEBOB

House and Senate Back Force in Iraq (October 10, 2002): House votes, 296–133, to give President Bush authorization to defend against the "continuing threat posed by Iraq." Senate approves resolution, 77–23.[4]

Basic Training/Infantry, Fort Benning, Georgia, September 24, 2002. Photo by U.S. Army, Fort Benning.

NOVEMBER 2002

"You're losin' it, Mom," Roman laughed, calling home from a pay phone one Sunday afternoon in the middle of his sixteen weeks of basic training.

Losing it? Just because I'd asked him if he'd heard from SpongeBob lately?

SpongeBob was the real live baby tortoise Roman bought and named a few weeks before he enlisted. The last of a long line of scaly creatures this reptile-expert son of ours had befriended through the years.

Now, as the turtle's interim caregiver, I had begun writing letters to Roman using the pen name "SpongeBob." Unlike the ones signed "Love, Mom," these offered news of home from a distinctly amphibian perspective. Sponge-Bob, after all, had an herbivore's unique appreciation for the vegetable garden Roman planted last spring on the side of the house. And a tortoise could write, "I'm proud of you," without sounding sentimental, because he'd always add something like, "I'd salute you, Dude, but, hey, my arms are too short."

To hear SpongeBob tell it, he and Roman were soul mates. Two guys in camouflage colors. One carrying around a forty-pound rucksack on long marches under the hot southern sun; the other, lumbering under a lumpy shell near a heat lamp and a food dish in a plastic tub in the guest bedroom.

Having decided to type SpongeBob's letters on the computer, I searched through the fonts on my system for something "turtle-esque." I experimented at first with a few typefaces that resembled cursive handwriting. But on the screen, those always looked far too elegant to come from a creature with a reputation for pooping in his food dish.

No. SpongeBob's letters called for an unpretentious font, one that was a little messy, and above all, youthful. Thanks to their long life-expectancy, tortoises stay young for several decades. In fact, it's probably safe to say Sponge-Bob wouldn't be qualifying for the Senior Lunch Special at Denny's until early next century.

The font called "Kidstuff" had just the right feel. I slid the cursor on the screen over to the word "File" at the top and pressed "Print." With its usual whirs and rumblings, the printer pushed out a letter signed "SpongeBob." I picked it up to check out the typeface in hard copy.

"That works," I thought, folding the letter in fourths and slipping it into a card-sized envelope. Then I rummaged through the top drawer of my desk for a felt-tip pen. I'm right-handed, but used my left hand to scrawl the letters and numbers of Roman's complicated Army address. The ink on the envelope smudged a bit, but that was OK. Good, actually. An additional touch of *veritas.*

I wanted our soldier to be able to tell this time and every time, wherever mail call might be, that here was another SpongeBob letter. Wanted each envelope to telegraph instantly that even in a post-9/11 world, moments of simple silliness were still possible.

~

Sunday, november 24, 2002

Hey, Wasssup?

How ya doin, Ro? I heard you called today. The phone rang, but I couldn't get to it. Wish I had an extension in here.

Your mom and dad were out and about. Gosh, you'd think they actually had lives or something. I heard them say they were going to Bates Nut Farm to get the ingredients for those fruitcakes your dad is famous for.

Thanksgiving is this week. I'm wondering if I'll get anything special to eat. I think I'd like to try some sweet potatoes. Maybe some cranberry relish.

What will you be up to that day? Will Uncle Sam provide turkey and all the fixins? Will there be entertainment? Will Jennifer Lopez be anywhere around? (I hate to be the one to break this to you, but I heard she got engaged to Ben Affleck—you know, that guy who kinda looks like you.)

Chargers lost today to the Dolphins. now they're 7-4. One week they look great, the next week they look awful. Guess that's life—ups and downs, or, in my case, ins and outs.

Well, guess I should wrap this up. When I think about things I'm thankful for, you are at the top of my list.

Have a good Thanksgiving, Bro. Treat yourself to an extra helping of mashed potatoes and gravy. You deserve it.

Yours truly,

SpongeBob

~

MID-DECEMBER 2002

I sat in the crowded bleachers set up in front of the barracks on Kinsman Drive in Fort Benning. On my left, Roman Sr. To my right, Anne, on winter break from school. The three of us had flown there from California for Roman's graduation from Advanced Individual Training. We hadn't laid eyes on him in sixteen weeks.

"Do you see him?" I murmured, scanning the four long columns of the three new companies of the 2nd Battalion, 19th Infantry Division marching in front of us.

"How would we know?" Anne answered.

She had a point. With their uniforms, shaved heads, and serious expressions, the recruits looked amazingly alike. I envisioned their drill sergeant barking earlier, "Any of you mama's boys dare to smile at your families out there, and it's one-hundred push-ups after the ceremony."

The marching soldiers stomped to a halt. In the first row directly in front of us, stood a young man who looked somewhat familiar. His shoulders were broader than I remembered. He seemed taller, too. His dark eyes stared ahead with a fierceness I'd never seen in them before. The thin line of his mouth didn't move, but all of a sudden, his eyebrows did. Up and down. Up and down. A covert "hi" for the three people in the bleachers who shared his last name.

My son, Private Groucho. Alternately tough and tender, with a shell of invincibility offset, now and again, by an unmistakable vulnerability. Hard on the outside. Softer within. The boy, the man, sharing the same olive-green uniform.

~

When Roman came home for three weeks of leave before heading off for his first assignment, a two-year tour of duty in Germany, I wanted to hear all about basic training. About the work and the food, the people he met, the things he learned.

Sometimes he'd open up and talk, more than he used to. One time he spoke at length about what the different bars of color meant above his uniform's jacket pocket.

"This one can only be worn by those who serve in time of war," he said matter-of-factly.

~

The day Roman left for Germany he and his dad and sister said their good-byes at home. A morning person, I volunteered for the 4:30 a.m. drive to the airport. We chatted a little in the car—about the emptiness of the freeway, the fog, his layover in Atlanta.

A hard rock CD—one of his, by Linkin Park—played in the background.

"I've been telling people for months I'm going to Germany, like it's no big deal. But now I'm actually doing it," he said, adding softly, "Weird, huh?"

Weird indeed.

At the airport, he was all business. He checked in at the ticket desk. Gave me a quick let's-not-make-a-big-scene-here hug. Put his backpack on the conveyor belt at airport security. Scooped it up on the other side. Striding toward Gate 38, he raised a hand and waved it, but without so much as a backward glance.

"He's gone," I thought.

My eyes fixed on the back of his head, I tried to reconcile myself to the push and pull of the thing called change.

I stopped waving. What was the point? Just as I did, I saw him turn and double back across the wide hall of the terminal. He stopped within about twenty yards of where I was standing. To get any closer, he'd have to answer to a security guard. At first I thought he must have forgotten something. But that wasn't it.

Roman had returned, instead, to snap my photograph. The camera hid his eyes. Mine—brimming then—had no such protection.

Back at home, I carried a plate of lettuce with an extra helping of shredded carrots over to SpongeBob. He poked his head out of that hard shell of his, blinked up at me and, I swear it, smiled.

~

from the plate of sponge Bob

Notecard from Roman's pet tortoise, SpongeBob. Photo by Sue Diaz.

Several weeks later, with Roman in Germany, I printed out another SpongeBob letter and carried it to the mailbox at the curb. Pulling up the little red flag on its side, I envisioned Roman sitting in the noonday sun against a tree somewhere in the forest near Baumholder. I saw him finishing an MRE (Meal, Ready-to-Eat), his weapon resting beside him. After the lunch break, he and his unit would be heading back to the artillery range. In the few extra minutes before they did, I imagined him taking out of his pocket an envelope with his name and address written in big, uneven letters. I saw him unfolding the page it held, reading it, shaking his head, rolling his eyes.

"Hey, Diaz. Don't tell me. Another letter from that turtle of yours?" I heard his buddy Davis say, rising from the base of the tree next to his.

"Yep," Roman answers, adding with a grin, "You know, Davis, you're just jealous 'cause your parakeet doesn't write to you."

And the laugh I imagined those two new friends sharing as they headed together toward a shooting range on a sun-dappled day, was as much about the mystery that is life, as it was about the absurdity of a tortoise's letters.

WAR

Powell Argues for War in Iraq (February 5, 2003): U.S. secretary of state tells Security Council that Saddam Hussein is an imminent threat to world security, has continuously deceived UN weapons inspectors, has links to al-Qaeda, and possesses mobile biological weapons factories.[5]

SUNDAY, MARCH 16, 2003

An SUV's doors opened and closed in the blacktop parking lot of Hilltop Community Park, and a few more people arrived for the "Peace Vigil." Maybe, like me, they'd learned of the event through a friend's e-mail. Or read one of the handful of flyers posted over the weekend around the neighborhood.

In the darkness at the end of a stormy day, they made their way past the sand and swing sets toward the gazebo behind the rec center. About seventy-five people in all. Families with small children. Clusters of older women. Couples. Teenagers.

And me. The mother of a soldier.

A new private in the 2nd Brigade, 1st Armored Division, Roman was at that moment stationed near the town of Baumholder, Germany. But that was soon to change.

"We're getting ready to be deployed," he had said when I'd talked to him on the phone the week before and asked what he and his unit had been up to lately.

"Deployed? Oh, really? Where?" I replied, fully expecting, because he was based in Europe, to hear something like, "Kosovo, for a few months of routine peacekeeping."

"Kuwait," he answered, to silence on this end.

"Mom, you still there? Mom?"

~

In matters of politics, my husband and I usually agree. A Sunday evening before an election will find us sitting in the family room, reading through our booklets from the California Registrar of Voters on the pros and cons of that Tuesday's choices. On most candidates and propositions through the years, we've voted as a bloc-of-two.

But when it came to the impending war with Iraq, we saw things differently. Like most Americans, Roman Sr. believed it was justified.

"That's OK, Susan. You go ahead. I'll have to pass on this one," he'd said when I invited him to come with me to the peace vigil.

That evening as I stood in the park above the high school campus where, less than two years ago, our son carried his backpack everyday, a full moon blinked out from behind a wispy veil of wind-driven clouds. In the distance, lights from the local shopping center twinkled: Blockbuster. Vons. Jack in the Box.

On a picnic table next to a man with a gray beard, a grocery bag rustled in the breeze. One by one people reached inside for a tapered candle and a paper cup.

"Here. Let me help," the man said, clicking a lighter toward the leaning candle one of the demonstrators held.

"Are you the leader?" she asked.

"Guess so," he shrugged. "The state organizers needed someone's name. I gave them mine."

The gathering was one of many across America that night, some more organized than others.

"OK. Let's, uh, make a large circle," the man with the gray beard said. And we did, though our circle ended up more amoeba-shaped than round. Each of the candles shined upwards from inside a cup, illuminating the face of the person holding it. With darkness all around, the people across the circle from me looked like they were lit from within.

I felt grateful for the right to assemble and protest my government's policies. And I was well aware that I owed that right to the brave deeds of those who had served in our armed forces in the past.

I supported our troops, but disagreed with the president. I didn't believe that bringing war to Iraq would ultimately make this world of ours a safer, better place. Gandhi was on to something, I thought, when he said, "We must be the change we seek." In the wake of a bombed-out Baghdad, those who have hated us in the past will have cause to hate us more. Violence begets violence. That is what I believed.

But that day in March, I hoped to God that I was wrong.

When I came there, I expected speeches, placards with antiwar messages, maybe even a minicam or two.

But there was none of that. Only this: Seventy-some individuals—moms, dads, kids, grandparents—standing quietly together under the vast night sky, each holding a single candle.

Five minutes passed. Then ten. And ten more.

No one said anything. No one moved. Even the smallest among us, the ones the playground was meant for, sensed that something important was happening. A little boy next to me, solemn in his sneakers, leaned against his daddy's legs.

After a while, a few women's voices tentatively rose in song—"Let There Be Peace on Earth" and the Latin "Dona Nobis Pacem"—but the idea of a sing-along didn't catch hold, in spite of some pretty good harmony.

The silence itself—interrupted now and again by the call of a seagull—made a statement far more profound.

Most astonishing to me was the fact that there was no one there, other than the demonstrators themselves, to witness the demonstration. And, oddly enough, that didn't seem to matter.

What did matter was this: On a blustery evening in the spring of 2003 a diverse group of ordinary Americans stood together for what they believed in, knowing full well that their flickering candles were no match for the winds of war blowing in that night from Washington and the Middle East, knowing that, but hoping still.

NOT A VIDEO GAME

FLASHBACK TO SPRING 2000

Explosions reverberated. One, then another. Followed by the rat-a-tat-tat of machine-gun fire and the guttural shouts of men in camouflage uniforms.

In the game on the computer screen in Roman's bedroom, Special Forces were on the move—darting down the dark streets and alleyways of a simulated city.

Like a lot of sixteen-year-olds in suburban America, Roman loved all things computer. He spent a good portion of his spare time designing a website devoted to information about reptiles, which he loved. I'd often see a frilled lizard or bearded dragon on the screen when I'd poke my head in his room to tell him supper's ready.

Seeing game images instead, I'd roll my eyes.

"Mom, I'm just taking a break," was his typical response. "This is a good game. See? My team's going after the bad guys. And check this out. The graphics on this thing are incredible."

Roman was right about that. With a few well-timed clicks, realistic-looking men dashed around corners, crouched behind walls, scanned courtyards for suspicious movements, took aim, fired. In the distance, enemies fell. The good guys regrouped and continued on. When they talked to each other, their lips moved, their eyes blinked.

"Amazing, huh?" he said.

~

Three years later, I watched another amazing display of modern technology: the war in Iraq on American TV, knowing that our own Game Boy and his unit with the 1st Armored would soon be heading to the front.

"Could be next week. Could be next month," Roman told us.

And so, as coalition troops amassed on the outskirts of Baghdad in late March 2003, I picked up the remote and clicked on the TV.

Through the miracle of videophones, I and the rest of the world were able to ride along as our tanks rolled across the Iraqi desert. We could be right there with the soldiers at the front lines in real time. Taking up our positions on family room sofas all across the country, we passed the potato chips and watched as real men in camouflage uniforms ran and crouched behind berms of sand. Up close, we could see their unlined faces peering out from behind the red-brown dust. Chins set. Eyes grim.

The cameras also took us inside Bradley tanks. And we rode along with guys who probably would have given anything at that moment to be back at home—surfing the Net, microwaving last night's pizza, programming their cell phones with girlfriends' phone numbers. Yet there they were, with so much of their lives still in front of them, on the road to Baghdad. It was not a Bob Hope movie. And it was certainly no game.

On the other side of the world, we, the people who loved them, watched, waited, and prayed they'd come home safe and soon.

For the most part, reporters and commentators did their best to treat this shock-and-awe war sensitively, to put the whiz-bang conflict we were witnessing, firsthand, into its human context. Early on, Nancy Chamberlain, the mother of one of the first American soldiers killed in action, reminded the media of their responsibility to do exactly that.

"I truly admire what all the new technology can do," she said. "But for the mothers and wives out there watching, it is murder. It is heartbreaking. We can't leave the television for a moment because we might see our sons or husbands."

From my corner of the couch, I watched as an embedded reporter talked via videophone about recent coalition losses. And as was often the case with this new technology, there was a brief glitch in transmission. In the grainy picture, the TV journalist appeared to move in fits and starts. Freeze. Then suddenly come to life again.

If only the fallen soldier, lying motionless in the top corner of the TV screen and shielded from full view by the backs of his comrades, could have done the same.

But I knew this war was for real. And Roman was going to fight in it.

MARCHING TOWARD BAGHDAD

SUNDAY, MARCH 31, 2003

The day was too pretty to watch Wolf Blitzer. The San Diego sunshine, too glorious for us to stay inside reading the news that relentlessly crept across the bottom of the TV screen: *Four soldiers killed in Iraqi suicide attack. Troops now forty-nine miles from Baghdad. Rumsfeld denies U.S. miscalculated strength of the resistance.*

"Let's turn this off," I said, reaching for the remote just as a familiar Suzuki pulled up to the curb in front of our house. It was the company my husband and I had been expecting—our friends, Sharon, Bob, and their little girl, Malia, down from the Los Angeles area for the day.

"So, what do you hear from Roman?" they asked first thing.

I told them the latest. How Private Diaz had called to say it looked like he and his unit would be heading for Iraq by the end of the week.

Even at age six, Malia knew that news wasn't good. She tilted her head, pooched out her bottom lip, held her mom's hand and listened. But being somber for any length of time was as foreign to her as the word "Nasiriyah" had been to the rest of us two weeks ago.

"Guess what?" she piped up. "I can read! Wanna see?"

Our plan for the day was to drive downtown and take the ferry to Coronado. But before we did, Malia carried a book she'd brought with her over to the family room couch, patted the cushion next to her, and said, "Sit here, Sue. I'll show you."

She opened to page one and began reading aloud the story of a boy on his way to his best friend's house for his first sleepover. The plot, such as it was, centered around the question: Should he take along the teddy bear he always sleeps with? And will his friend think he's a big baby if he does?

As Malia's finger moved from word to word, my thoughts traveled back to another six-year-old who used to read aloud with me or his dad or his sister on that same couch.

~

"Speed limit forty-five," Malia said, pointing to one of the street signs on the way downtown. "All Day Parking," she continued. Then, "Ferry Landing." And a little later, as we all sat on a sea wall sipping canned sodas, she sounded out, "Pep-si."

The eastern breeze blowing across the bay was warm; the seagulls, chatty; and the sand at our feet, fine as baker's sugar.

Plastic cup in hand, Malia busied herself making what she called "mud pies." On her trips to the water's edge, she skipped between the sand castles of other families and the side-by-side towels of young lovers.

From a patio in front of the shops behind us, four musicians played for an appreciative crowd. Some clapped. A few dropped coins into a hat on the sidewalk. Others danced. Two gray-haired women in sun visors laughed at their own public attempt to remember how to jitterbug.

A tiny dog on a leash trotted by. A mother on a picnic blanket plopped potato salad onto her children's paper plates. Out in the bay, sailboats, catching the wind, skimmed across the water. In the distance beyond the harbor, a Navy destroyer waited.

Our group of five had no agenda other than being together in a beautiful place on a Sunday afternoon. A plan, it seemed, shared by everyone there.

"Ice cream," Malia said, taking a mud-pie break to read yet another sign, this one on a shop nearby with a line stretching out the door.

I had to believe that at that moment our troops in the Middle East would have wanted to know that scenes like that were still happening. That in spite of the headlines on CNN, families picnicked, ice cream cones dripped, and Frisbees bravely flew. That back on the home front there were people playing saxophones or talking politics or passing ketchup or simply smiling at a kid sounding out every new word she saw. In the face of countless "in spite of's," life, indeed, goes on. In wars in the past, many—so many—have given their all so that it can.

～

That evening back at home, we stood outside, saying good-bye to Sharon and Bob and their precocious little girl.

"Look," Malia said, pointing overhead, "The Big Scooper." She meant the Big Dipper, but no matter. It was the same northern constellation seen in night skies from Boston to Baghdad.

With a hug and a wave, she climbed into the back seat and buckled her seat belt. After a few more hugs, doors closed and the car pulled away.

Back in the family room, my husband and I clicked on the TV once more. Images filled the screen of American soldiers in Iraq. Words crawled across the bottom: *Pentagon stands by battle plan; coalition forces closing in on Baghdad.*

I watched and wished I could send a signal to those soldiers on the screen. In fact I did send a signal, with all the focus my mind and heart could give. It was a screen for them to watch, and in it were everyday scenes such as the ones my husband and I had enjoyed that day, and across the bottom of that screen these words scrolled: *We're still here. Come home soon.*

SEVEN DUCKLINGS

Pentagon Says Fighting Mostly Complete (April 14, 2003): After the fall of Tikrit, Saddam Hussein's hometown, officials declare the end of the brutal regime.[6]

APRIL 2003

I didn't see them at first.

Too many other things competed for my attention at the mid-city intersection where I sat waiting for the light to turn green: The streaming line of cars, trucks, and SUVs in the street in front of me. The high price of super unleaded at the corner station. The hot dog special at the convenience store on the right.

I could barely hear the radio, what with the noise of the cross traffic and a construction crew's jackhammer at work in the store's parking lot.

I'd been listening for the latest from Iraq. Roman was still in Germany that afternoon; his unit's expected departure for the Middle East had been delayed. But a newly issued pair of desert boots, he said, rested near his rucksack.

That day's news sounded positive, as if the war might actually end soon and without the lengthy street fighting, heavy losses, or the biochemical nightmare many had predicted. For weeks I had been afraid—for Roman and for the rest of the world, too. And while waiting to see how the war would unfold, I found myself watching too much CNN and putting life on pause.

With the fall of Baghdad looking like it was near, I began to feel something close to hope. And it felt good, there in that intersection I'd driven through so many times before, every few weeks, in fact, when Roman was in middle school and his orthodontist had an office up the street. Yesterday, it seemed.

Back then I'd been the kind of mom given to gasps if my son or daughter hung for any length of time from the monkey bars. The kind of mom who couldn't fall asleep on Friday nights until both teenagers were home. "Call when you get there" often punctuated my good-byes as they grew older.

But foot soldiers at the frontlines do not carry cell phones.

Just then a big Vons truck, brakes groaning, made a tight turn into the lane on my left. And through the aftermath haze of its exhaust, I spied, close to the ground, something that looked like an apparition.

"Can't be," I thought, staring.

But it was.

A family of ducks. Well, not the whole family. A single parent and seven fluffy ducklings, each no bigger than a softball.

I saw the last one jump up from the street to the curb. Now all eight huddled together on the sidewalk in the shadow of a Mobil sign, tail feathers twitching. The ducklings were still at that stubby-wing stage where the idea of flight was nothing more than a fantasy. Waddling, wriggling, tumbling was the only way they had of getting from point A to point B.

And it obviously got them to where they were at that moment: a busy street corner in the middle of a business district. Not a pond in sight. What on earth had possessed them to take that route?

I hadn't witnessed the drama of their trek across the street. Caught only the tail end of it, literally. Somehow that daring Phalanx of Feathers had made it safely to the other side. Danger had threatened at every turn. Disaster seemed imminent. Yet in spite of that, they'd obviously managed to put one webbed foot in front of the other, sidestepping potholes, pedestrians, and all that traffic. Against all odds, there they were, beaks bobbing, waiting for the next sign to flash "Walk."

And I wondered, *Were they some sort of sign?*

Who can say? But I decided to see them as one nonetheless. A sign that spelled out in small, fuzzy letters a message that was good for a soldier's mom to see that April day: *Yes, life is crazy and unpredictable, but it can be kind, too.*

Then the light turned green. And with the tap of a horn from the car behind, I eased my foot off the brake and moved on.

ANSWERING THE CALL

Large Allied Force to Remain in Iraq (May 28, 2003): Commanders say troops to stay to stem violence beyond Baghdad. Decision in response to death of four U.S. soldiers by resistance fighters in one week.[7]

Against the leather of the inside of this box, the single sheet of yellow paper stands out like a daisy on a sand dune. I pick it up, unfold it, and remember. It came from one of the letter-sized legal pads I always keep handy on the desk where I do most of my freelance writing—ads, brochures, features, and opinion pieces. But the words I'm looking at right now are unlike any I've ever written. The handwriting is mine. But it's the words, the words that are different.

They're not mine. They belong to Private Diaz.

He was in the Middle East that May morning he called, the morning I wrote these words on this pale yellow paper. His unit had arrived in the desert staging area of Kuwait a week earlier, just after Baghdad fell. When we talked, the region was far from stabilized.

"We'll be leaving here soon. We're already packed. So this will be my last call for a while," he said. "There are no phones where we're going. No Internet either."

"And where's that?" I asked.

"Can't say. It's a secret," he answered, continuing with a laugh, "Come on now, Mom. If I told you, I'd have to kill you."

With some coaxing, I did learn that he and the rest of the men of Bravo Company would reach their ultimate destination fifteen hours or so after their convoy headed north.

"Does the place start with a 'B'?" I pressed.

"Mo-om," he answered with feigned exasperation. During his years as a teenager, I'd often heard the real thing. Back then it had been my job to ask the questions. "Homework finished?" "What time does the movie end? "Who's driving?" And it was his job, or so it seemed, to answer with as few syllables as possible.

But the day Roman called, he wanted to talk.

"Is Dad there?" he asked.

"No. He's at a biotech conference today."

Several months earlier my husband had been laid off from his job as Director of Engineering at the big computer company where he'd worked for twenty-seven years. Downsized, along with the rest of the department, when the project they'd been working on was cancelled. He'd been looking for work since then, and dreaming, too, of starting a company that develops software for the biotech industry.

"Dad's not there? Shoot," Roman said, adding in a voice that trailed off, "There's something I really need to talk to him about."

"Can I help?" I asked.

No answer.

"Roman?"

"Well, OK. I guess so," he sighed.

I waited for the rest and wondered what it could be.

"Got a pen, Mom?"

"Yes."

"And a piece of paper?"

With each question, his voice gained authority.

"Yup. Right here," I said.

Then he told me what he hadn't wanted to tell me. How he'd taken out a life insurance policy for $275,000, the maximum the Army offers.

"Now, if anything happens to me, here's what I want done with that money."

I jumped in to stop that kind of talk. What mother wouldn't?

"Don't be silly," I sputtered. "Nothing's going to happen to you! You'll stay safe. And when you come home, you'll have lots of stories to tell. Some day your grandchildren will ask about the time—"

He cut me off.

"Mom, please. Just write this down."

And so, cradling the phone between cheek and shoulder, I took my son's dictation, writing first a few words about his big sister: "Pay for Anne's college." Then a line about taking care of me. And finally, a phrase for his father: "Help Dad start his company."

"Did you get all that?" he asked.

"Yes," I whispered.

"Good."

We chatted a few minutes more. Maybe it was about the weather or the food or the fellas he now hangs out with. I don't remember. My mind was still reeling with a changed reality; my heart twitching with a strange new sadness and a growing pride.

When I'd answered the phone, I heard the voice of the boy I used to remind to eat his vegetables and pick up his socks, the same kid who balked at wearing a bike helmet, the teenager who played his hard rock CDs way too loud. I said "Hi, Roman" to all of those guys.

But that day it was a man I said good-bye to.

BOTH SIDES NOW

War became my Dr. Jekyll. Just three months into it, and I felt changed in ways that weren't always obvious. Friends seemed to think I was still the old me—even-keeled, optimistic. I wanted to be. Tried to be. But a certain Mrs. Hyde—I came to think of her as Lucinda—had unpacked her suitcases in my soul. And she was, well, somethin' else.

Somethin' else? Somethin' else! Cut the bullshit, Sue. And don't start patronizing me either. I'm mad as hell about all kinds of things and at all sorts of people—Osama bin Laden, George W. Bush, and sometimes even my own son!

What can I say? That's Lucinda.

～

It was a Saturday morning, not long after Roman and his unit began their patrols near Baghdad, and I was out having breakfast with Kathy, a friend I'd known since we were freshmen together in college. Kathy is one of the kindest, most genuine people on the planet, and had been like an aunt to Roman from the day he was born.

"How are you doing?" she asked, reaching across the table to give my hand a sympathetic squeeze.

Lately I'd been on the receiving end of all sorts of sympathetic squeezes, sad sighs, patronizing pats—from friends, acquaintances, even a grumpy neighbor who before this time had rarely said more than, "Good morning." Such displays of concern were well intentioned. I knew that. But Lucinda, who tended to view those gestures as a subtle way of saying, "Gee, sorry your life sucks right now," came *this close* that morning to giving Kathy's hand a slap.

"I'm doing OK, Kath. You know, all things considered."

"Oh, Sue," Kathy said, the two words sounding like descending notes in a minor scale. "Really?"

What's with that tone of voice? It's like you're offering condolences or something! Knock it off! Roman's very much alive—and has every intention of staying that way!

"I had a chance to talk to Roman last week," I told Kathy. "And it always helps to hear his voice."

Eyes glistening, she answered, "Well, just know that he and his buddies are in our prayers."

"I appreciate that."

I did. Really.

Hey, mothers in Iraq pray for their sons' safety, too!

A little later, Kathy and I settled into the easy give-and-take we'd always enjoyed about husbands, work, books, relationships, politics, and our kids. And she shared with me her considerable angst over—of all things—her daughter's recent nose piercing.

You're bent outta shape about THAT?! Are you kidding? I ask you, Kathy— Did your daughter feel the need to take out a life insurance policy on her way to shop for nose studs?! I've got no patience anymore for all you parents and your everyday complaints. Listen to yourselves, will you? You say your teenage boys spend way too much time playing Xbox games?! Your daughter's changed her major—for the fourth time? Your fifth-grader needs orthodontia? Your middle-school daughter wants a Wonderbra? DO YOU HAVE ANY IDEA HOW LUCKY YOU ARE TO SWEAT THE SMALL STUFF?!

The waitress refilled our coffee cups a couple more times, as Kathy and I continued the conversation we'd kept up for more than three decades. Most of our lives. In that time, we'd talked about a lot of things—large and small. And I could hear my soldier-son saying, like he used to when he was a teenager, "Hey, it's all good." At least that was my take that day on Lucinda's rant: All of it matters, all of it, more than we know. And we should, in fact, feel free to sweat the small stuff, but with a larger awareness, a deeper appreciation of the miracle of every ordinary day.

Damn right, Sweetheart, Lucinda snapped. *That much we owe those guys over there.*

BROTHERS IN ARMS

The picture captures an impossible pair: two soldiers, my father and my son, both nineteen years old, standing together in an overgrown backyard on the south side of Milwaukee.

I created the composite photo in May 2003 on the screen of my laptop. Printed it out that same spring day. It was homework for an adult-ed class I was taking in Adobe PhotoShop, the software program that makes it possible to blend and alter photos in the most amazing ways.

Using what PhotoShop calls the "Lasso" tool, I'd lifted Roman's image out of a picture taken a few months earlier at his graduation from basic training, made the necessary color and size adjustments, and placed him next to my father in the sepia-toned snapshot I'd scanned into the computer. In that photo, Dad's arm had been draped around his mother's shoulders. On the screen, I moved Roman into her place, lassoed and repositioned my father's hand, and just like that, Frank T. Bindas held his grandson in an embrace that reached beyond the boundaries of time.

Lanky, square-jawed, and each with ears that stick out a little too far, the two could be brothers. Their eyes in the photo I'm holding smile up at me now. That day in Milwaukee, my father's eyes had not yet seen the churning red surf of the beaches of Normandy, the shattered cities of Europe, the hollow faces of concentration camp survivors. Those sights were yet to come, followed in time by good things, as well: World War II's end, a long and happy marriage, three kids, a career in accounting and management, a passion for local politics, and a scant two years of retirement in Sun City West, Arizona.

Dad died after a brief battle with cancer just before Roman started kindergarten. So my son's memories of him are few and sketchy: after the long drives to Arizona from our home in San Diego, he remembers the gentle way Grandpa tossed the Frisbee to him in a backyard dotted with cactus and oleander.

Pvt. Roman Diaz and his maternal grandfather, Frank T. Bindas.
Photo by Sue Diaz.

How he tasted pickled pigs' feet for the first time the afternoon his grandfather said, "Here, try a bite, Roman. The men in the family like this."

Of the memories I have of the two of them together, one in particular lives on in my mind. It was the day of my father's funeral. The Mass had ended. The pallbearers had taken up their positions, and with measured steps, were carrying the simple, silver casket toward the back of the church. They had just passed the pew where my husband and I stood with both kids. Suddenly, Roman shot out into the aisle, as if someone had pushed him. I was the person next to him. And it wasn't me.

The soles of his Sunday shoes slipped a bit on the marble floor. He looked surprised. Then he turned and scampered up the aisle. Catching up with the procession, he put his small hand on the side of the coffin, and, blonde head bowed, walked with the gray-haired men who carried his grandpa.

In this composite picture I'm holding, they are together once again. And the connection they share goes far beyond the toolbar of PhotoShop. The uniform each wears joins them in a bond, a brotherhood I can't possibly comprehend. What do I know of war? I remember how my father used to describe it. "War is hell," was all he'd say when he talked about it, hardly ever.

As bombs began to fall on Iraq that spring and we learned that Roman was headed there, I closed my eyes and heard those three words once again, as clearly as if Dad were standing right beside me.

DAD'S D-DAY DIARY

Kathy, my older sister, mentioned our father's D-Day diary off-handedly in a long-distance call.

"Whoa! Wait a minute!" I said. "Daddy kept a diary when he was in the war?"

"Yeah. One of those government-issue things. Small enough to fit in a back pocket."

"And he actually *wrote* in it?"

I remembered my father as a doer, not a chronicler. A reader, not a writer. Essentially, a man of few words. Sure, I'd often heard him, my mom, and their friends talking politics and Green Bay Packers as they leaned against the rec-room bar he built in the basement of the home where I grew up. But around his three daughters, he could be almost shy—a genial foreigner in our world of Toni home permanents, Beatles songs, and nylons hanging like Spanish moss over the bathroom shower rod.

I asked Kathy to send me the diary.

A week later, the book arrived. I ran my fingers over its creased, blue leatherette cover, opened it, and searched for this entry near the middle: "June 6, 1944. Arrived on D-Day, invasion day on the shores of Normandy, France," my father wrote. "Was strafed by the 'Jerries' that day. Stayed near the beach area for a few days and found things to be really hot."

That's all he wrote about what must have been the scariest, most horrific day of his life, a day that changed the course of the war and with it, the history of Western Civilization.

"Found things to be really hot" was all that that young soldier in the Seventh Corps could bring himself to write.

I continued reading, entry by entry, looking all the while for what I considered the real stuff of history—the whine of bombs, the heat of combat. A few of my father's diary entries touched on such things, but only briefly.

In early July, for instance, he wrote, "Spent in a fox hole. Plenty of noise and one of those Fourth of Julys I hope I never have to spend again."

On November 22, he noted, "Buzz bombs came over all day."

But for the most part, my father's wartime diary chronicled a different kind of story. One filled with the beauty of distant hills and farmers' daughters. Letters and cookies from home. The news that the Browns beat the Cards, 2-0, in the first game of the World Series. The joy of the liberated Belgian people:

"Shall never forget this day and the welcome we received," he wrote on September 5. "Rode in an open car. People came running and shouting, 'Viva La Amerique,' getting in our car, hugging and kissing us, throwing flowers, apples, pears, plums, confetti, beer, champagne, extending their hands for us to shake. People were so happy."

Then, with the formality I recognize as my father's, he said, once again, "I shall never forget this day."

One snowy January afternoon in Belgium my father and a friend hiked to the top of a hill for the pure pleasure of it. "Took pictures when we arrived at the top where there was a crucifix and got a wonderful view of the town."

Describing a few days he spent on leave in a hotel in Brussels, Dad noted with obvious delight the "hot and cold running water" and a "real bed with foot-thick mattresses and clean white sheets."

In early February 1945, he received a "Dear John" letter from his girlfriend back home. Her name was Dolores, like my mother's, but she's not my mom. And the jilted soldier wrote, "Hope I don't have too much trouble getting over it, but somehow or other, I think we will both see things in the same light."

Lucky for me they didn't.

Growing up, I'd always thought of my father as a good, hard-working man—soft-spoken, private, unemotional. I knew him as someone who loved a thick T-bone, Glenn Miller's music, and us—mom, me, and my two sisters.

But there was more to him than that. Reading his diary, I saw him as a cockeyed optimist, a young soldier who somehow managed to view the glass as "half full," even when it was, in fact, completely shattered. Like so many of his generation, Dad was no stranger to the horrors of war, but he chose to focus instead on the things in this crazy life that are worth fighting for.

I prayed his grandson would do the same.

GROCERY SHOPPING WITH LUCINDA

Bush Speaks of Dangers in Iraq (June 21, 2003): In the first comments about continuing deaths of U.S. soldiers in Iraq, president says Hussein loyalists trying to "kill and intimidate" Americans.[8]

s that Sharon? Matt's mom? Over there by the frozen seafood? Damn. She saw us. Now she's waving.

"Sue! Is that you?" Sharon boomed in that grating voice I remembered from pack meetings back when our boys were Cub Scouts together. As if grocery shopping hadn't been hard enough lately without bumping into Mother of Wonder Boy.

I'd started putting off trips to Vons as long as I could. Just the thought of it made me tired. Too many memories, there among the apple juice and Cheerios, the hot dog buns and peanut butter.

"Long time no see!" Sharon continued, bustling down the aisle in my direction.

When Anne and Roman were little, shopping for groceries was actually kind of fun. They thought so, too, especially when, in an attempt to make our weekly routine more of an adventure, I'd started giving them a cart of their own and a list with about a dozen or so things to find and choose together: an ice cream treat, a pack of paper towels, a bunch of ripe bananas, a good cereal.

They were about eight and six at the time. Pint-sized consumers like that can learn a lot behind the wheels of their own grocery cart: cooperation, decision making, not to mention independence.

And as I pushed my own cart through the store, I'd keep track of where they were mostly by the music of their voices—talking, giggling, sounding out words on labels, and occasionally debating the relative merits of Cocoa Puffs vs. Cap'n Crunch. Their definition of "a good cereal," not exactly the same as mine.

"What's it been, Sue? Eleven years?"

"At least!"

Actually Sharon, not long enough.

Matt and Roman used to have a lot in common. They were equally skilled at making breadbaskets for their moms out of Popsicle sticks. Both could burp with abandon upon request (usually each other's). And Matt's handcrafted car for the Annual Pinewood Derby, like Roman's, exhibited a pretty sophisticated grasp of aerodynamics, especially for a nine-year-old.

"So, what's Roman up to these days?"

Military service was not a common post-graduation choice for the children of this suburb where backyard pools were as common as biweekly visits from Molly Maids. I knew the answer I was about to give would come as a surprise.

"He's joined the Army."

Seconds passed.

"Really?! The Army? That's, uh, *interesting.* I, uh, I never would have guessed!" Her tone was as patronizing as it was smug. "And what's his job? Wait! Don't tell me! I bet it has something to do with technology."

"He's in the infantry . . . in Iraq."

Sharon nearly dropped her fish sticks.

"Well, now! That's really, uh . . . something. Good for him!"

No, Sharon, war isn't good for any mother's son.

"And how's Matt?" I asked perfunctorily, more than ready to move beyond her euphemisms and into the next aisle.

But she was in no such hurry, especially now that she had an opening to talk about her Golden Boy. He's on scholarship at University of California, San Diego, she gushed. Majoring in biochemistry! Met his girlfriend—a wonderful girl—through a church group on campus! He's planning to go to med school! They both are!

Well, Sharon, isn't that just peachy?!

Matt's mom was just warming up, I could tell. She certainly had every right to be proud of her son. And I knew I had reasons to be proud of mine. But the life-and-death danger of Roman's days colored my outlook. With the future so uncertain, and the present so damned scary, the good news of others was sometimes more than I could bear.

"Oh, gosh, look at the time!" I interrupted, tapping my watch. "Love to hear more," I lied, "but I gotta get going." And before anyone could say, "Let's do lunch," I rumbled toward the checkout counter, minus the milk I'd come for.

A RARE SNAIL-MAIL LETTER FROM ROMAN

Bush Administration Admits Iraq Weapons Intelligence Was Flawed (July 7, 2003): Says evidence that Iraq was pursuing a nuclear weapons program by seeking to buy uranium from Africa, cited in January State of the Union address, was unsubstantiated and should not have been included in speech. President maintains war in Iraq was justified.[9]

JULY 2003

Dear Ma, Dad, and Anne,

It's about time I wrote you folks a letter. How goes it you guys? I hope everyone is doing well. Enjoying all the outstanding freedom civilian life has to offer. How's SpongeBob? Say "Hi" to the little guy for me. Tell him I'll be home soon for some quality soldier-tortoise time. Actually, I have no idea how long I'll be here or when I'm going home. But for a tortoise, I think ignorance is bliss. I'm hangin' in there though. The heat is terrible but we've finally moved into a place with working electricity! So now we have fans blowing . . . keeping our "AO" [Area of Operations] a pleasant 90-degrees during the day. It's not as bad as it sounds. Our pa-

trol schedule has gotten a lot better. At first things were brutal. We did 2
patrols a day, 4 hours each, on foot. When we weren't patrolling, we
pulled guard on the compound. 12-hour shifts. Yuck! That's about it for
us. We have missions in between there, too. Maybe I can tell you about
when we get back . . . and like I said, I don't know when that will be. I've
heard rumors about February as a leave date, but they're just rumors.
Could be more, could be less. I think about it all the time though—going home. Eating home cooked meals with fresh foods in a beautiful and
climate-controlled house surrounded by people I love. And then maybe
hopping into Dad's Acura for a smooth comfortable ride to the movie
theater to catch the latest flick. The whole time in clean, good smell-
ing clothes. I'm not sure how secure I'll feel w/o my gun on me. But
we probably won't encounter any RPG's or AK-toting civilians on our
way. Come to think of it, there won't be any gunfire at night. Only the
sounds of crickets and nice cars as they speed down the 4-lane highway
next to the theater. After the movie I'd like to head downtown to en-
joy the bright lights and neon glow from all the fancy restaurants and
clubs. Stopping at Fumari for an hour or two. Sipping coffee and bs-ing

*Left to right: Roman Diaz Sr., Sue Diaz, Anne Diaz, and Erick Armbrust, toasting
Pvt. Diaz from Café Sevilla, Downtown San Diego, California, July 2003.*
Photo by Sue Diaz.

about the great times I had overseas. . . . And to think, I used to do this stuff on a regular basis! I really can't wait to get back from this world of violence and uncertainty. Drenched in sweat and caked in dirt. Eating my 2 MRE's a day, trying to relax before my next shift on gate guard, or next patrol, or next checkpoint. . . . Damn, that sounds horrible. Really, things are much more bearable than you think. Plus I get plenty of mail to keep me happy. If you decide to send another box out here, and you don't have to, your letters are good enough, these are some things I'd like: 1.) Powder Gatorade. Drinking nothing but water is getting old. 2.) Hot sauce! The El Pato you sent really made my day . . . anything but Tabasco. 3.) Sardines or smoked oysters. Those make a good snack any time. 4.) Canned tuna snack kits. You know, the ones with mayo and crackers? Those would be outstanding. 5.) Canned menudo. Small cans would be best . . . but some menudo? I would be the envy of my platoon! 6.) Doritos/Cheetos/snack things that come in those plastic cans. The first five items are better, but these would be damn good too. I'm not asking for these things, but if someone wanted to send me a package, those are ideas. I'm going to wrap this up. Thanks for all the support you guys have shown. You don't know how much it means to me.

Love, yo' baby boy,

Pvt. Diaz

P.S. Since there is all that good food and nice restaurants to eat in where you are, I want you to take out money from *my* account and have a nice dinner on me. . . . When you write back, I want to know where you went, and a picture of you having a good time.

THE SPONGEBOB LETTERS
I

December 4, 2003
Hey there big guy!

SpongeBob here. Just wanted to say hi and update you on life in the quiet suburb. Thanksgiving went off without a hitch. I had lots of company that day. The young people would

Thanksgiving 2003, Left to right: John-David Wiese, Jamie Zakoski, Lilia Munroe, Bob Zakoski, Carmen Wiese, John Wiese, Roman Diaz Sr., Grandpa Diaz, Erick Armbrust, Anne Diaz, Doug Munroe, Irma Diaz, Kathy Zakoski, Vanessa Robberson, Bryce Zakoski. Photo by Sue Diaz.

all kind of wander over here and hang out. This was definitely the cool room, the "in" place to be. Chillin' with yours truly.

Heard you called that day. Everybody was talking about that. Smiling a lot about it, too. Man, what'd you say to those people? Musta been good, that's all I can say. Wish someone had thought to carry me over to the phone!

Your mom might have, but she was up to her elbows in giblets, and stressing about things like serving forks and where to put all those pies your relatives kept showing up with. Oh, well.

Now everybody is talkin' Christmas. Your dad started making his famous fruitcakes. I wouldn't mind trying some of those bright green cherries sometime. With you there in Baghdad, the holidays here will sure feel weird. Bet there aren't too many Noble Firs where you are. And you probably don't hear the Mormon Tabernacle Choir singing "Little Drummer Boy" or that Burl Ives guy singing "Have a Holly, Jolly Christmas" as background music in the stores over there. Which, come to think of it, is probably a plus.

Well, bro, I'll sign off for now. Take care of yo'self. I can't wait for you to come home. Can't wait to sit on your shoulder again, which I hear is bigger and roomier than ever.

You da man. I da turtle.

SpongeBob

BAGHDAD CHRISTMAS

"Peace on Earth," holiday cards in the Hallmark store said. But for many people near the end of 2003, it was an empty phrase. There was no peace, in more ways than one, especially for those with sons or daughters, wives or husbands, serving in the Middle East.

~

Roman's unit moved around a lot, so we heard from him only occasionally. When we did, a line in an e-mail might tell of watching tracer fire across a sandy expanse or of waking up to the boom of mortars. Dan Rather sometimes kept us up to date on Roman's division. "Two soldiers from the 1st Armored were killed today by a roadside bomb south of Baghdad," he'd say to lead off the evening news.

In one online conversation Roman wrote about the strange dichotomy he and his buddies felt at times in their role as both liberators of the Iraqi people and fighters against the insurgents. He didn't use the word "dichotomy." His words were more vivid than that:

"I don't know how many times we've been on raids, and we'll be searching the house. One person pulling security on the men of the house, and one on the women and children. They'll offer to make us tea, or ask for a picture (if they see a camera), and for a while we chill out in their house and play with the kids. It's especially weird if we meet with resistance on the way in. I always bring candy in my pockets and bullets in my chamber."

~

Last holiday season Roman was home for a while, looking forward to his two-year assignment in Germany scheduled to begin in early January.

Four embroidered Christmas stockings—Roman's, Anne's, mine and Roman Sr.'s—hung from the mantel on opposite sides of the living room fireplace. Among the gifts I'd tucked into Roman's stocking were two pocket travel guides: one for Germany, one for Europe.

From Washington, talk of war grew louder every day, but Roman's conversation then was still more likely to focus on possibilities like weekend train trips to the Alps or meeting pretty German girls eager to practice their English.

He liked planning what he was going to do with his paychecks. Foreign travel ranked right up there with trips to Fry's Electronics. And like a lot of guys his age, he was happily into acquiring "stuff," especially the stuff that comes with owner's manuals, or better yet, a remote control.

Those three weeks of leave were a good visit for the most part, but hard, too. Life's in-between times always are. He was quieter than usual. Restless, too. Home seemed to be little more than the place he was oh-so-ready to leave. Sometimes at night he'd go out for a long walk, and return with the smell of a cigarette still on him. Nineteen and invincible, he gave little weight to those health warnings from the Surgeon General, and even less to mine.

~

"Anything in particular you'd like for Christmas this year? Lots of people ask me what they can send. What should I tell them?" I typed to Roman in Baghdad via instant messaging, the program that lets people "talk" in real time using their computer keyboards.

"Let's see. Let me think. . . . No. Nothing, really. I have pretty much what I need here."

"Come on now. It's Christmas!" I pressed.

"Hmmmm. Well, there is one thing . . ."

"OK."

"What me and the rest of the guys like most is getting letters. Not a card someone just signs. But a letter. A real one."

He went on to say it could be about anything. "Anything at all, Mom."

The weather. Work. The kids next door. The latest Charger loss. Saturday's movie. Last night's fish tacos. He even went so far as to say he'd welcome more news from his grandmother about her trips to the podiatrist.

"Letters from home," our Material Boy wrote. "Really, that's the best gift we can get right now."

A little while later he typed that it was time for him to go. Staring at his sign-off on the screen, I swallowed hard.

"Peace," was all he wrote.

A HOLIDAY TRADITION

"Peace" was a recurrent theme in the homemade Christmas cards our family sent each year. A few of them have found their way into this leather box. I pick up the one from 2003, Roman's first Christmas in Iraq. The image of my husband and me that I'd PhotoShopped on the front of it—our grown-up heads on little elf bodies—is far from serious. But in a world that felt out of whack, the funny shoes and floppy stocking caps I'd put us in seemed fitting somehow.

This tradition of handcrafted cards began on a day in early December back in 1986.

"Here, Anne, can you draw a picture on this for me?" I'd said, handing our five-year-old a piece of typing paper I'd photocopy onto card stock later. "Anything that makes you think of Christmas."

"Anything?"

"Whatever you want. Santas. Trees. Elves. Sleighs. Ornaments. Angels. You name it."

Sitting at a little molded-plastic table in the family room, holding a pencil in her dimpled hand, Anne began to draw. Typical of kids her age, it was a process that seemed to involve moving her tongue as much as her pencil.

"OK, Mommy. Done," she said a few minutes later, skipping away and leaving a picture of a smiling girl in a triangle skirt. A youngster with no neck to speak of and a forehead larger than Michael Jordan's, offset only by a ponytail swinging at the back of her profiled head. Standing on tiptoes, the girl was either catching or throwing a big gift-wrapped box. Hard to tell, since the package was suspended in mid-air, just beyond her eager, elbowless, stick-finger grasp.

Through the years, the card-making process stayed the same. When Roman was old enough to hold a pencil, he, too, got the chance to give Hallmark and his sister some competition. Each year, half of the people on our list received his version; the other half, Anne's. This annual craft project continued even when they were in high school.

After the kids were out on their own, I decided to carry on the tradition myself, not with pencil sketches and Magic Markers, but with PhotoShop, an affinity for elf pictures, and an annual letter to family and friends, like this one from Christmas 2003:

> *Hope this note finds you well and happy.*
>
> *In a number of ways, for us it's been a challenging year, this year. But as you can see from the front of this card, we're still standing. (In funny-looking shoes, but still standing, nonetheless.)*
>
> *Roman Sr. continues to pursue his dream of starting his own software company for the biotech industry. Getting it off the ground has been more difficult than he'd thought, but in the meantime, he's working the angles, laying the groundwork, and learning all he can about things like ribozymes and retroviruses.*
>
> *I've been doing more of my usual—writing ads and essays, teaching, volunteering, and taking classes, too. (PhotoShop—the program that lets you manipulate photos and images—was one of those classes, as you might have already guessed.)*

The beginning of a tradition. Anne Diaz's first homemade Christmas card, 1986.

Anne graduated in June with a degree in Urban Studies. She's living in the Bay Area now, working as the tutor coordinator for a literacy program that's run through Stanford.

Young Roman, always full of surprises, joined the Army in September of 2002. Initially he was based in Germany, and was looking forward to things like weekend train trips to European capitals. But George W. Bush had other plans for the guys in his division, the 1st Armored. Since May of this year, he's been stationed in Iraq. Baghdad, to be exact.

So this year, it seems, the words "peace on earth, good will to men" are much more than a line in a carol's chorus. May the spirit of the season be with you and those you love—now and in the year ahead.

Peace,

Sue and Roman Sr.

A TASTE OF HOME

His first Christmas in Iraq, Roman spent most of the day on duty in one of the several guard towers that poked above the tin walls of his forward operating base's meandering perimeter. The tower, a combination of plywood, leaning 2 X 4's, and sand bags, had a makeshift quality to it. And as he climbed the ladder to his post, he could feel the whole thing sway.

On dry days the dirt in that area of Baghdad has the consistency of confectioner's sugar. But when it rains it turns into a slippery goo. It was raining that day, and cold, he told us later in a phone call. With his boots covered with mud, Roman's trek up the tower's ladder was even trickier. To add to the challenge, he carried—in addition to his weapon—a red-and-green package, about the size of a brick and nearly as heavy. It had arrived in a care package from home a few days earlier and was still gift wrapped, but he knew what it was.

Roman didn't usually bring presents from home with him to guard duty. This was a first. But their sector had been quiet for weeks, the four hours up there would be long, he was only twenty, and it was Christmas Day.

Arriving at the top, he nodded to a soldier already there from another unit, and set the package in a somewhat protected corner. Sandbags, stacked four feet high, formed a kind of wall around them. It was their job that day—

Roman's and his colleague's—to stand behind that wall with their guns close at hand, peering out across the adjacent river, scanning the banks for anything suspicious.

The wind-whipped rain came at them from all angles. Front. Side. Even from above—where the plywood roof had warped and cracked, and the water dribbled in.

Somewhere in the middle of that watch, Roman reached down for the package he'd set in the corner. He placed it on a soggy sandbag. Peeled back the Scotch tape on both ends of the wrapping paper. Then he pulled out the foil loaf pan, and as he removed the plastic wrap that covered it, he caught a boozy scent of apricots and a glint of Day-Glo cherries. It was the homemade fruitcake, his dad's specialty, that had been part of every Christmas he'd ever known.

Folding back the foil, he broke off a few crumbs. Popped them in his mouth. Broke off a few more.

"Hey, want some?" he called over to his comrade.

And while carols were sung and stockings hung on the other side of the world, two soldiers from the States kept watch by the banks of the Tigris, in the wind and the rain, sharing every last bit of what was, Roman told us, the best fruitcake he—or anyone—ever tasted.

THE SPONGEBOB LETTERS
II

December 29, 2003
Monday

Yo, Bro,

SpongeBob here. It's been a crazy week. Rumor has it you could say the same thing.

It started with my going over to The Downey's house while your mom and dad went to Arizona. I know someone has to feed me, and Colin is a pretty good guy for the job. He doesn't just toss a bunch of lettuce into the enclosure. He talks to us (me, and three others of the turtle persuasion) while he does it. Calls us by name. Asks how we're doin'. Sticks around to watch us munch. You can tell he'd much rather watch us eat than do his homework or any chores his mom might have thought up for him to do. (You know how moms are.)

So my couple days there went off without a hitch. I didn't really mind chillin' with those other guys, though I kept pretty much to myself. Which wasn't hard to do, given that my "bachelor pad" is on my back.

You know me, Pfc D., I'm basically a no-frills kind o' guy. Food. Hide box. Heat lamp. And I'm cool.

A few weeks ago I noticed there was a new kind of greenery in the living room. It looked like something I'd eat for lunch, until your parents started hanging stuff on it, stringing lights all over it, and putting presents under it. What's up with that?

Some kind of holiday, I guess. But I refuse to do any celebrating whatsoever until you're back here with ol' S.B. We'll par-tay har-tay when you come home. I won't even think about hissing. I save that for people who aren't you.

Your sister's home again. And sleeping in my room! Not just sleeping, but doin' other stuff—like talking on the phone and blow drying her hair. Chicks. Can't live with 'em. Can't live without 'em. I hissed at her a few times, just to remind her whose room it is.

Heard some talk that you've been pulling some pretty difficult missions lately. You are a whole lot braver than me, dude. That's for sure. If I were in Iraq, I'd probably never come out of my shell, not even to hiss. I'd just do my best to look like a rock or maybe a mini-Bradley. Think I could pull that off?

Heard that you and our country's other soldiers have been named "Person of the Year" by Time magazine. Way to go, bro. To me, you've always been and always will be "Person of the Year." Last year. Next year. And the next. And the year after that. Don't forget, I probably have close to two hundred years ahead of me. And for all of them, you will be on the cover of December's "Time Magazine in My Mind."

There I go again. Gettin' all sentimental. I'll blame it on sharing a room with that sister of yours.

Lates.

SpongeBob

WEAPONS OF MASS ILLUSION

U.S. Deaths in Iraq in 2003: 482
Wounded: 2,408[10]

The picture of the young soldier stayed with me that day. And the next. I can see it still.

On a morning in January 2004, his photo appeared near the bottom of the first page of Section B in the *San Diego Union-Tribune*. The headline with it read, "County native, 20, killed in Iraq, believed in what he was doing."

Just before turning to that section, I'd read another story nearer the front page. In that one, David Kay, the former chief weapons inspector in Iraq, said that after months of searching, no weapons of mass destruction had been found.

"I don't think they existed," were his exact words.

I thought about that, as I studied the small color photo that accompanied the headline about the fallen soldier. I let my eyes rest on the set of his jaw and the seriousness in his eyes. He looked as if he believed a fierce expression would somehow offset the smoothness of his face. That if he managed to look tough enough, no one would notice that so much of life still lay ahead of him.

He had joined the Army, the article said, in response to the September 11 terrorist attacks, and that he had been killed by mortar fire on a base thirty-five miles northeast of Baghdad. People who knew him said, "He felt he was doing the right thing in a hostile land."

"He seemed to be proud of that," the boy's father said. "We're finding some peace in that somehow."

I knew if a similar fate were to befall Roman, I would never know that kind of peace.

I'd been against this war from the beginning, but Roman and I rarely talked politics. Yet he was the one who, in an online conversation not long after he'd been on the ground in Iraq, brought up the topic of the policies that put him and his unit in a round-the-clock war that had no clear battle lines. "What were those guys in Washington thinking?" pretty much summed up the way he was starting to view the war.

When he joined the Army, a paycheck, not patriotism, had been his prime motivation. That, plus the promise of adventure and time to figure out what he wanted to do after the four-year stint he'd signed on for.

Before his division got its orders for the Middle East, he made me laugh— he liked doing that—with the story of how he and his buddies had fine-tuned a new technique for meeting girls and making travel plans.

"Sometimes when we get a couple days leave, my friends and I will throw a change of clothes into a backpack and go hang out at the train station. When we see some girls we'd like to meet, we go up to them and say, 'So, what train are you waiting for?' No matter what they answer, we say, 'No kidding! That's where we're going, too!' Then we buy our tickets."

The frontlines of life, not history, were where he wanted to be.

He grew up a lot in his first few months in Iraq. And he would probably have agreed that he needed to. There were other positives, as well. I sensed his pride in his ability to handle the situations that came with being in a combat zone. He was learning that he could cope as well as anyone with the chaos, the boredom, the bad army food. And for all those down-to-earth reasons, I was proud of him. I admired the courage it took to keep putting one dusty boot in front of the other on the uncertain roads he walked every day.

But I never believed the administration's claims that Iraq posed a direct threat to America's security. Never believed that the war would be worth its cost—in dollars or in lives. I viewed the Bush policy of preemption in Iraq as, at best, a large-stakes gamble in geo-politics that was simultaneously arrogant and naive, or at worst, all about oil.

And when I saw newspaper photos of the young Americans the war was bringing home in flag-draped boxes, I saw other pictures, too: the ones that would never be taken—of weddings and birthdays and all those other moments life gives us to say "cheese." And the toll of this conflict became as vivid to me as the piercing brown eyes of the soldier in Section B.

American to my core, I saw photos like his day after day and felt many things. Against the backdrop of David Kay's revelations, the least among them was pride.

THE FAMILY ON THE BEACH

We were sitting in our car, Roman Sr. and I, parked near the beach, watching the sun slide below the wall of granite-gray clouds rising up from the long line of the horizon out where the ocean ends. It was a beautiful evening. There at sunset the shore was awash with muted pinks, pale yellows, and opalescent grays. Drained of daytime color, this seaside world of breaking waves and wet sand shimmered like the inside of an oyster shell.

It was chillier than when we headed out to dinner earlier that evening. We didn't think then to bring along jackets or sweaters. So instead of walking off our desserts along this favorite stretch of beach, we decided to take in the scenery from the comfort of two bucket seats, to hear the call of gulls through the car's open sunroof.

Nudging my husband's arm, I nodded toward the young family ambling into view a few yards from the water's edge. A mom. A dad. A little girl about five. A boy who looked to be three.

The dad, jacket collar turned up, stopped to peer out at a big ship dredging sand about a half-mile offshore. The mom's gaze wandered from the setting sun to the seagulls overhead to the floppy cloth bag she'd set down in the sand.

From the bottom of this bag, the boy pulled out a plastic shovel and promptly set to work—digging, scooping, patting. His sister, all knees and elbows and Buster Brown bangs, saw that as her cue to perform for any beachcombers who'd care to watch what appeared to be The Dance of the Purple Leggings.

The boy's intense focus, the girl's dramatic flair reminded me of our two kids some seventeen years ago.

"Remember when Anne and Roman were that age?" I said.

"Barely," Roman Sr. answered with a soft laugh.

"Where does the time go?" I wondered.

I couldn't take my eyes off that family. And for an instant, there was no such thing as time. There was only Life, leaving its footprints on the beach. And at that moment, all that mattered was those four people—with their zippered jackets and plastic shovels, their windblown hair and sand-filled sneakers. And that family was us—me, my husband, our daughter, and son. And we were them.

They didn't know it, but I'd be there when they arrived back home—when the dad brushed the sticky sand from between his son's fingers, and the mom poured a couple capfuls of Mr. Bubble into the warm, running water of the tub in the kids' bathroom. When the light from the lamp next to the family-room sofa fell on the pages of that night's bedtime story, I would be there. In truth, I already was.

We watched as the family started to leave the beach. The dad scooped up the toy bag and reached for the girl's hand as he turned to navigate the small incline that led toward the cars. The little boy, still clutching his shovel, lifted both arms toward his mom. She picked him up. He wrapped his legs around her waist, rested a cheek on her shoulder. Faces expressionless, they shuffled past our parked car.

In Thornton Wilder's *Our Town* there is a character, Emily, who asks in that play's final act, "Do any human beings ever realize life while they live it?" Wondering that very same thing, I felt impelled to pop up through the sunroof and call after those strangers, "Stop! Pay attention! Look, really look, at one another!" I wanted to tell them, "Tomorrow your little girl will be a coed at a university hundreds of miles away! The day after that, your son will join the army. Before you know it, you'll have a condo in Sun City and five grandchildren! Stop. Stay. Look. Really look."

Of course, I didn't say any of that. Instead, my eyes followed them all as they headed toward their car and home—toward days, nights, and years that would, I knew, pass far too quickly. But they couldn't have known that. Not that evening. Not the next week or even the next month. I pictured that mom and dad fifteen years in the future. Looked ahead to see them driving to a nearby beach to watch the sun slide below a wall of clouds rising up from the horizon out where the ocean ends.

There they notice a young family stopping near the water's edge. And for a short while that holds within it echoes of eternity, they find they can't take their eyes off that strangely familiar foursome. And without a word, they watch the long, end-of-day shadows stretching toward them across the sand— of a little boy and a dancing girl and a floppy bag of beach toys.

NOT SO FAST

Iraqi Mob Mutilates Four Americans (March 31, 2004): Civilian contract workers shot and then dragged through the streets of Fallujah.[11]

The photo, full of light, movement, and color, is beautiful. In it a small group of Iraqi children are skipping, laughing, and running on a dirt road near Baghdad. At the center, a boy waves a newspaper high above his head. In the low sun of early evening, the children's long shadows fan out

In Iraq on the day Saddam Hussein was captured, December 13, 2003.
Photo by Roman Diaz.

in the direction of the person taking the picture. The photographer, a kid himself not all that long ago, was Roman.

He'd snapped the photo from the back of the Army vehicle he was riding in the day Saddam Hussein was captured—December 13, 2003. He used a small digital camera. Tucked it into a pocket of his uniform that wouldn't get bumped by the machine gun it was his job to carry.

In the e-mail that arrived with the photo as an attachment, Roman, who typically began his Internet messages with "Yo," wrote with a maturing sense of life and history: "It is a time of great hope here in Iraq."

Looking at that photo, I, too, began to feel some hope that the war would, in the long run, turn out OK.

The feeling didn't last.

Four months later, that hope hid in shadows dark as the smoke from burning Humvees, black as the charred bodies dragged through the streets of Fallujah.

~

EASTER SUNDAY, APRIL 13, 2004

Roman and I were talking online. A month earlier, he had told me and his dad not to send him any more care packages, cards, or letters, because his unit was scheduled to leave Iraq soon. They'd been there nearly a year already, and were looking forward to heading home in the next couple weeks.

But the news out of Iraq continued to get worse. Every day brought new images of fist-shaking, gun-carrying mobs. Radical Shiite clerics urging on a growing insurgency. Kidnappers in ski masks. Cowering hostages. Bloodied men in desert khaki. Bandaged children in hospital beds. Liberation, it seemed, had a new meaning.

"What's it like for you guys these days?" I typed on my computer screen.

"Tiring, hot, dusty, chaotic at times," Roman wrote, "It's like the whole country here has lost its mind."

"Well, all I can say is I'm glad it's near the end of your time there."

The box where his words would appear on my screen stayed blank. I watched it and waited for his reply.

"Mom," he finally typed, "Don't make me say it."

Pfc. Roman Diaz and his unit in Iraq heading out on a mission, spring 2004.
Photo by Roman Diaz.

My heart jerked. He'd confirmed what I'd read the day before in the newspaper—that some, not all, of the 1st Armored would soon be getting orders to stay on three to four months longer. I chose to believe my boy wouldn't be among them. But he was.

I blinked back tears in order to keep reading, and let the conversation shift to other topics: The weather. His recent promotion to the rank of specialist. SpongeBob's latest antics. Our Easter plans at Aunt Irma's. Jokes about government-issue jelly beans.

"None of those for us today," he wrote. "No celebrations. Just showers, hot chow, clean clothes. That's enough for us after this week."

A little later I typed, "I'm always hopeful things will turn out better than we think."

His response echoed the disillusionment more and more Americans were feeling. The disillusionment that came from learning there were no weapons of mass destruction, no direct links to al Qaeda, no imminent threat.

"I try not to have any expectations," he wrote with a weariness well beyond his twenty years. It was a statement so at odds with what he said the day he snapped the sun-streaked photo of those happy Iraqi kids, it was hard to believe it had been taken just four months earlier.

And I myself was light years away from the days when I could make the world right again for him with the promise of a 7-Eleven Slurpee. For the families of those with loved ones over there, I sensed that victory in that misbegotten war might come down to simply this: holding on to hope that our brave men and women over there would come back to us whole.

"You guys will get through this," I said.

"Yes, we will."

"And so will your mothers."

"Yeah. And wives and kids, too."

A few lines later something called him away suddenly.

"Gotta go, Mom," he wrote, and was already offline before I could finish typing, "I love you."

THE SPONGEBOB LETTERS
III
(This One to Roman's Friend, Specialist Davis)

Dear Spc. Davis,

Heard through the grapevine (or, in this case, the lettuce leaves) that you were kind of wishing you had an amphibian pen pal like some other people you know. (Hint: a certain tall soldier with brown eyes and menudo breath.)

Well then, this is your lucky day. To tell you the truth, I'm pleased and proud to have the opportunity to write to another soldier in the service of his country. You guys are really something special.

Heard you're from the Midwest. Michigan, is it? The woman who fixes my salads everyday grew up in that part of the country. She knows all about things like snow and wind chill.

Guess you don't get much of that where you are now. I heard that over there you sometimes get temperatures in the 130-degree range! To me, that sounds great. Like the whole world is your heat lamp.

Here's something else I heard: you and me could have the same hairdresser. Or, to put it another way, neither of us needs one. Our "look" is really popular these days though. Just ask Bruce Willis or Jesse Ventura. (And, hey, chicks think it's sexy, too.)

I'm running out of room here, so I'll sign off now. Keep up the good work. On behalf of America and amphibians everywhere, I salute you and all our brave guys over there. When you come back to the States, come see me. It would be an honor to share my carrots with you.

All the best, Dude.

SpongeBob

P.S. Tell Diaz I said "Yo."

SERGEANT HORTON'S MARLBOROS

MAY 2004

Late at night somewhere near Baghdad, Roman once again sat typing on an Army computer. His words, as he typed them, appeared on the screen of the laptop in Anne's bedroom in Northern California, where it was mid-morning.

I was relaxing with a book on the couch in her living room, in the middle of a four-day visit, and could hear the intermittent click-click-click of their online "conversation." Back and forth it went, punctuated suddenly by a soft gasp from Anne and a whispered, "Oh, no."

Roman Sr. stopped in his tracks in the hallway near her door.

"What?" I heard him ask her, and then, "When?"

I heard the answers, too. So when Roman added a little while later, "Don't tell Mom, OK? She'll only worry more," it was too late for Anne to keep her brother's secret.

I already knew that a few hours earlier a roadside bomb killed Sgt. Jeremy Horton of Bravo Company, 2nd Battalion, 6th Infantry Regiment—Roman's unit. And in that same explosion, another soldier lost a leg. And still another, an eye.

I thought back to how, in recent months, he had told us that his company had developed a reputation for being invincible.

"Bridges blow up *after* we cross them," he had boasted. "Mortars land in barracks we just left."

Unlike other companies of the 1st Armored Division, Roman's hadn't lost a single infantryman in all the time they'd been on the ground in Iraq, nearly a year. But in one red-and-black instant, Bravo's reputation, like the vehicle its Sergeant Horton had been riding in, had been blown to bits.

Roman's squad hadn't been assigned to the convoy that night. When the bad news came, he told his sister, with what I can only surmise must have been an incredulous shake of his head, he had been reading a magazine back at the base.

And knowing that I wasn't supposed to know any of this, I let my imagination fill in the blanks that Google and CNN.com couldn't. And I imagined, not so much the immediate aftermath of smoke, metal, and bodies—it was just too hard to go there—but the quieter aftermath of the days and weeks that followed. What would it be like, I wondered, for the soldiers who saw the whole thing happen in a side-view mirror on that road near al-Iskandariyah? Or for the ones who heard the news over a cup of mess-hall coffee, or while trying to forget the war for a couple hours with a DVD or a magazine?

Before that morning, whenever I'd read headlines like "U.S. Soldiers Killed in Attack" I never really considered the ripple effect on those they'd been serving with. It was only natural to focus on the fallen and their families, and not on those other soldiers who would open their eyes the next day to see an empty cot across the way.

But the news of Sergeant Horton got me thinking about them.

And those thoughts take me to their barracks now. Sifting through this box of stories, I'm back there again, watching once more the soldier whose job it is to gather up Jeremy Horton's things. I see him tuck a couple of unopened envelopes into the stack of well-worn letters in the sergeant's footlocker, and watch as he removes snapshots of family and friends tacked to a wall near the cot. The soldier, all-business up until that point, just sits for a while after taking down the last photo: a smiling twenty-something woman leaning against a uniformed shoulder. I envision an inscription in the corner of that picture, "To my husband," it says, "with love."

Most of the sergeant's things will, no doubt, be packed up and sent to his wife in Erie, Pennsylvania. Some of the stuff—cookies, chocolate bars, and that last carton of cigarettes—will be shared with his brothers on the base.

"Horton would have wanted you to have these," I hear the squad leader say as he hands a box of Marlboros to a private notorious for bumming smokes.

And now I imagine one of those cigarettes glowing between his fingers a few nights later as that private heads toward his unit's Humvee. He'd been saying he plans to quit smoking, but as he takes his place in the vehicle, he isn't thinking about that. Instead, in the minutes before he and his buddies go out on another mission, he can't help but think about what happened the Friday before, about the people in his company who are no longer there, and about others who lived half a world away. Gazing up at a star-filled sky, he takes one last drag of Sergeant Horton's Marlboro, and at that same moment, a young widow in Pennsylvania lets out the deepest of sighs.

Part Two:
AT HOME AND BETWEEN DEPLOYMENTS

COMING HOME

Sept. 11 Panel Contradicts White House (June 16, 2004): Committee investigating terrorist attacks against the U.S. reports no link between al Qaeda and Iraq.[12]

AUGUST 2004

"There he is!" I said to my husband.

From the top of the escalator in Terminal 2 at Lindbergh Field, Roman waved at the two of us waiting below. Waved not just his hand—the one that wasn't gripping the strap of a backpack—but his whole arm. In that first glimpse of him, it was his face I focused on. The smile that played across it hinted at what I longed to know: *He's still him.*

When Roman reached us, I wrapped my arms around him in a long and happy hug. His father did the same. Lazarus's mom and dad in the New Testament could not have hugged their boy tighter.

"Whoa! Hey! Glad to see you, too!" Roman laughed.

Taking a step back to take in all of him close-up, I finally did notice one thing that was different about him from both elbows down: a line of tattooed Latin words, including *bellum* and *pacem*—"war" and "peace."

Forty years ago as I sat in Sister Agnes Clare's fourth period class translating Virgil's *Aeneid*, little did I dream that words from that epic war poem would one day come in handy in reading my son's arms.

"Well, Mom, what do you think?" Roman grinned, butting the knuckles of both hands up against each other so I could see the entire line of inch-high letters that stretched in front of me from left to right. SI VIS PACEM, it said from elbow to wrist on his right arm. PARA BELLUM, from wrist to elbow on the other.

"What do I think? Well, uh," I stammered. "It's definitely, uh . . ."

There were several words I could have used to finish that sentence diplomatically. "Latin" was one. "Blue" was another. I settled for "interesting." After all, how many mothers' sons have the subjunctive clause in *If you wish for peace, prepare for war* punctuated by a wristwatch?

Sue and Roman celebrate his homecoming. Photo by Sue Diaz.

Truth is, I wasn't thrilled with those "tats," as he called them. What mother would be? It occurred to me that that sentence could be cause from now on for people who didn't know him well to misread him. No, I wasn't thrilled with the tats. But I was thrilled to have him home. And that trumped everything.

Roman's tattoos were low on the list of things my husband and I talked about before sleep that first night our son was home. But the topic did come up.

"Look at it this way: at least he still has arms. Considering where he's been, we should be grateful for that," Roman Sr. said from the pillow next to mine. And I had to admit, it was a matter of perspective. Specialist Diaz would no doubt have agreed that wars have a way of changing our view of the world and our own place in it. Maybe his tattoo was intended to be, for him, an indelible reminder of that.

As for me, recent months had illustrated, more clearly than ever before, what a mixed-bag life can be, with its hopes and disappointments, worries and relief, heartaches and joys—both little and large.

The ancients probably had a word for all that. Four decades after high-school Latin, I couldn't remember it for the life of me. But Sister Agnes Clare might be pleased to know that the opening line of Virgil's epic war poem has stayed with me all these years.

I sing of arms and the man, the tale of the warrior Aeneas began. And as the mother of a soldier home at last, I decided that that's what I would do, too.

A SEPARATE PEACE

The glowing red numbers of the digital clock near my side of the bed read 1:23. Wide-awake, I lay there listening for the front door to open. It was Roman's second night back in California, and he was out with a couple friends he'd known since grade school.

"Jonny and I are going over to Nicole's. OK, Mom?" Roman said, after the party that officially welcomed him home had wound down, after the deli platters in the dining room were bare, the salsa bowls empty, and the homemade Oreo Cookie Cheesecake little more than a sweet memory.

In the many months his unit was based in and near Baghdad, I'd often watched this clock's red numbers flip toward morning. A certain amount of sleeplessness is an inevitable part of parenthood. But things like colic and missed curfews, I realized during Roman's deployment, can't hold a candle to roadside bombs and Shiite militia.

When he was still in Iraq, he had initially said "No way" to the whole idea of us throwing a party when he returned. He'd always been a quiet kid, more comfortable in front of his computer than in front of a crowd. That partly explains his reaction. But it must have been hard, too, for him to imagine a room full of "Welcome Back" balloons, while he was still in the midst of falling mortars. Or to envision red-white-and-blue streamers fluttering in our living room, when only the week before, one of his Bravo Company buddies went home in a flag-draped box.

The party question had come up again in a phone conversation shortly after he arrived in Germany for two weeks of debriefing before flying home to California.

"A party? Well, OK. Sure. I guess," he said.

~

The second night he was back in San Diego, waiting to hear him come home, I replayed it all. The garage-door banners up and down our street. The hugs. The smiles. The flowers. The *merengue* music from the stereo in the family room. The way the slanting rays of the setting sun backlit and burnished the whole happy group of friends and neighbors on the patio.

I saw him again, standing there in the middle of a cluster of men, telling them the story of the day he was chased by three camels on a dusty road. For comic effect, he did an imitation of those animals' faces just before they spit.

"I'd run faster. They'd run faster," he had said, pumping his arms as if he was still running.

The men laughed, but the group grew quiet as he related how in an effort to leave those camels behind, he made a sharp turn off the road and into a field of scrub and rocks, only to notice that the ground around his feet was also dotted with land mines the enemy hadn't even bothered to bury.

"Whoa," one of the guys said solemnly.

"Yeah, I know," Roman answered.

And I sensed then that there were other stories from this war that he might never tell.

~

At 1:36 the front door finally creaked open. When Roman still lived at home and got in this late, I'd sometimes catch him slinking past our room on the way to his.

But tonight he headed here first, opened our bedroom door, and came right in. From the vantage point of my pillow, I saw a tall shadowy figure stride past the dresser, turn left at the foot of the bed, and come to a halt inches from my side.

"Roman?" I murmured.

In the darkness, he slowly bent toward me. His hand found my cheek, and I felt his lips press against my forehead.

"Love you, Mom," he whispered.

Before I could blubber anything in reply, he was walking around to the other side of the bed, and leaning down to kiss his sound-asleep dad.

Our soldier had returned. One homecoming of thousands across this country since the war began. And even though it wasn't over—in Iraq and over here—I closed my eyes, and for the first time in a long time, I knew what peace feels like.

THE SPONGEBOB LETTERS
IV

October 2004

Yo, Spc. D!

SpongeBob here. I hear you're back in Germany, land of bratwursts and mosh pits. And that you're back in the barracks again, and in your own room with a new roommate.

I can't tell you how glad I was to see you when you were here in San Diego—and I was your roommate. It was great to hang with you.

I remember the first afternoon you were home. It was just like I knew it would be. You took me out in the back yard. I kept heading for the bushes (no relation to George W. and his family), you kept walking over to turn me around. The sun was shining. The UV rays were awesome. And best of all, every time I looked over at the patio, there you were. With your illustrated arms and everything. I didn't think a turtle could get much happier than that.

And then, I did! When you built me my new home!

I have so much more room to roam now. In the mornings I'll sometimes take a hike to the corner near the window. On the way, I'll stop to soak up some rays from the heat lamp. Stretch my neck a bit, too. Then when it's lunchtime, I'll hightail it over to the plate near my hide box and get lost in a mound of lettuce for a while.

· Haven't seen all that much of your mom lately, except when she drops another armful of lettuce in here (I do eat a lot, don't I?). I hear she's been busy with a slew of new clients. Good for her. And now that you're out of the war zone, she's more relaxed. Her step is lighter. (Sometimes I don't even know she's in the room, until I hear those baby carrots hitting my plate.)

She is so grateful that you are back from Iraq. "Safe and sound," as she says. "And so strong and handsome," she'll add.

Guess you could say the two of us have a kind of "Spc. Diaz Fan Club" going. It's one thing a tortoise and a mom can agree on.

Anyway, gotta run—and thanks to you, Dude, I actually have room to do that!

Yours in a couple inches of substrate,

SpongeBob

CHRISTMAS CARD, 2004

Season's greetings! This past year has been a memorable one. In August "Little" Roman, AKA Specialist Diaz, returned home to San Diego—safe, sound, and in many ways stronger—after more than a year in Iraq. He's been stationed in Germany since then, but will be assigned to a base in the U.S. in January.

In October Anne got engaged to a wonderful young man, Erick Armbrust. And this marriage proposal happened in spite of the fact that he's well aware of her family's history of, er, unusual Christmas cards. (He's the elf next to her.) They met at the university three years ago and are planning a September wedding.

"Big" Roman has already started lobbying to appear at least four-feet-tall on next year's card. In the meantime, the two of us keep on keepin' on—

learning, working, writing, speaking, teaching, volunteering, and taking time, now and then, to "stop and smell the roses" or the ocean air at Torrey Pines—grateful for the blessings 2004 has brought. And hopeful, as always, there are many more right around the corner—for us all.

Love,

Sue and Roman Sr.

A NEW ASSIGNMENT, ANOTHER TRIP HOME

U.S. Deaths in Iraq in 2004: 849   Total since the war began: 1,331

Wounded in 2004: 7,988   Total since the war began: 10,396[13]

JANUARY 2005

I peeked into the sunny bedroom at the end of the hall, and for a moment, it seemed as if the last two years had never happened. As if Roman had never joined the Army. As if he'd never been deployed to Iraq. Because when I glanced over at the desk in the corner, there he was again—in blue jeans and T-shirt, hunched in front of his computer, a bottle of Dr Pepper near his right hand, yesterday's socks scattered on the floor. But in place of his old high school backpack, a weathered green duffle bag now leaned against the wall.

"Hey, Mom," Roman said catching a glimpse of me at the bedroom door. "Come here. Check this out."

He wanted to show me the small computer he had bought, packed, and sent here from Germany, where he'd been based the past six months. The new orders he'd received a few weeks ago were sending him now to the 101st Airborne in Fort Campbell, Kentucky. That would be his next stop after the ten-day leave he was on here was over.

Roman's infantry unit with the 1st Armored had the distinction of serving the longest deployment of any division in Iraq. And now, according to a recent Pentagon announcement, soldiers from the 101st Airborne—where he's headed—"will make up a significant part of U.S. forces in Iraq and Afghanistan starting in 2005."

Roman's unit in Iraq. From left to right: Spc. E. Ramirez, Spc. T. Davis, Pfc. G. Vinyard, Pvt. Rike, Cpl. "Jay" Johnson, Pfc. R. Diaz, Ssg. D. Herd. Photo by Roman Diaz.

We didn't talk much about the likelihood of his return to the war. Instead we chatted that day about his computer. Its speed. Its size. Its amazing graphics.

"And what are those?" I asked, pointing to two on-screen icons labeled "Iraq I" and "Iraq II."

"Pictures I took when I was over there," he said.

"Can I see them?"

With a couple clicks of his mouse, the digital slide show he created began, and its images are seared in my memory: Hovering helicopters in silhouette against a deep-red sunset. Acres of confiscated mortar shells, AK-47s, rifles. Humvees with no doors. Buildings with crumbling walls. The head of a child's doll lying in the dust, its plastic face blistered, its tiny ears singed. The back seat of an empty car, mottled with stains the color of terra cotta tile. A spider hole, half-hidden by brambles.

"The hole Saddam *didn't* crawl out of," my son said with a wry grin.

The only other times he smiled were at pictures of his buddies in Bravo

The day after a nightlong firefight in Iraq. Photo by Roman Diaz.

Company. Before each of those photos faded into the next, he'd hurry to name every one of his comrades, even though from most distances, they all looked alike to me—with their army haircuts and their desert khakis.

"That's Ramirez. Davis. Vinyard. Sergeant Herd. . . ." he said, touching the screen again and again with the tip of his finger. As if I would remember all their names. As if he could ever forget.

Off in the distance in one of those group shots, I couldn't help but notice black smoke coiling into a blue sky.

"Were there any places over there that you'd walk through the streets and say, 'Nice neighborhood'? You know, like here?" I asked.

"No. Not really," he said, shaking his head. "Not anymore."

Just then a tight close-up of a big, bright-yellow sunflower filled the screen, and just as quickly, disappeared.

"Wait. Go back," I said. And when he did, I added, "Where'd that come from?"

"The flower? I took that picture one morning after the warehouse we'd been holed up in had taken a lot of enemy fire. It seemed so weird to come out and see something so pretty still standing in the middle of . . . well, in the middle of all that."

And on the screen, more snapshots from that dusty corner of hell continued.

Roman left a few days after that slide show on another plane that took him to Kentucky, but the improbable beauty of that sunflower stayed with me. And I vowed that throughout whatever might lie ahead for Roman, I would hold on to the stubborn hope embodied by that bloom, embodied, too, by the young man who, after one particularly long night at his post in Iraq, put down his machine gun to point a camera at its petals.

MOMENTS TO REMEMBER

Spc. Diaz at the wedding of his sister, Anne, and Erick Armbrust, April 23, 2005.
Photo by Matt Kim.

APRIL 2005

Theirs was a different sort of rush to the altar.

After Anne and Erick became engaged in October 2004, they initially set their wedding date for late September 2005. But when they learned that Roman would, most likely, be back in Iraq by then, they scrambled to move the date up—to April 23—so he could be in the wedding party.

In spite of the small window of time to put plans in place and caterers on notice, it all came together beautifully. A wonderful day, shared with 160 friends and relatives. Vows under a gazebo in the tree-lined courtyard. Bach in the background. A candlelit dinner in an adjoining hall with tablecloths the same rose-color as the bridesmaids' dresses. Good wine. Good food. Anne and Erick dancing their first dance to the Beatles' "In My Life." Tears and smiles all around, mixed with memories and hopes.

A hug from Grandpa Diaz at the wedding of Anne Diaz and Erick Armbrust, April 23, 2005, Los Altos, California. Pictured from left to right: Carmen Wiese, Spc. Roman Diaz, Grandpa Diaz (also named Roman), and Dolores Deutsch. Photo by Matt Kim.

Earlier that evening, near the end of the dinner, Specialist Diaz, in full dress uniform, rose from his chair to take his turn in offering a toast to the bride and groom.

He would go on to clear his throat and say he was "a man of few words." He would nod to the newlyweds and teasingly call them "Noosch and Cutie"— their nicknames few knew. He would acknowledge the specialness of the day and all the people who had gathered there "from as far away as Florida and Palo Alto." And he would call on us all to celebrate the union of his sister and the man she loves.

But before Roman could say any of that, he had to wait for the end of the ovation that had started the moment he stood up. From the back of the room to the long head-table at the front, spontaneous applause began and grew, intended for the young man with the champagne glass in his hand, insignia on his sleeve, and surprised look on his face. A hug he could hear. Beaming, Anne and Erick joined in. It was their wedding, but it was Roman's moment to feel the love.

COMING HOME ONCE MORE
TO SAY GOOD-BYE AGAIN

General Says Insurgency Still Strong in Iraq (June 23, 2005): Contradicting recent statements by Vice President Dick Cheney that the insurgency is in its "last throes," General John Abizaid tells Congress that the strength of the insurgency is about the same as it was six months ago.[14]

JULY 2005

"Whatever it is, let's be cool about it. We can act like we don't even notice," I suggested.

My husband and I were on our way to the airport to pick up Roman. He was coming home to San Diego for ten days before heading back to Iraq.

In a call shortly before we left for the airport, Anne told us we were in for a surprise. Roman had just spent a few days in the Bay Area visiting her and

Erick. The only clue Anne offered was that the surprise had something to do with her brother's hair.

"Now, Mom, just keep in mind where he's been and what he's going back to. Who can blame him right now if he just wants to have a little fun?"

"New color?" I guessed.

"You'll see," was all she'd say.

～

Roman's height alone would have made him easy to spot, standing there near the curb in front of the terminal. His hair made him impossible to miss. There's something head-turning about a Mohawk—even when it stands no more than an inch-and-a-half high—especially a bright red one, with the tips dyed black.

"Oh," his computer-engineer dad gulped, catching sight of him.

"Oh, my," I elaborated.

But after a curbside flurry of car doors opening and a couple quick hugs, to Roman we simply said with all the nonchalance we could muster, "Welcome home!" and "Good to see you!"

On the drive back I turned from time to time in the front bucket seat to ask him about his flight from San Jose, his weekend with the newlyweds. His dad chatted offhandedly about the weather, asked about the soldiers in the unit our son was leading. "My Jedi," Roman called them.

But there was an elephant in the room. Twenty minutes into the trip, I could ignore it no longer.

"Hmmmmmmmmm," I said, twisting to look at Roman full on. "I can't quite put my finger on it. But something's definitely . . . *different.*"

"Hmmmmmmmmm. What could it be?" he teased, fingertip touching one corner of his smile.

～

A few days earlier I'd given friends and neighbors a flyer announcing our soldier's brief visit home and inviting them to come say "Hi" at a block party barbecue on Sunday in the cul-de-sac. The same place Roman had learned to ride a two-wheeler.

A recent picture of him graced one corner of the photocopied invitation. Smiling in his dress uniform, complete with medals, ribbons, and the blue cord of the infantry, he looked handsome, clean-cut, all-American. His hair was dark brown, not Day-Glo red. In the photo, it still grew on the sides of his head.

The former PTA mom in me wrestled at first with what the neighbors would think. I wondered if I might convince them he was actually a member of an elite, top-secret special-forces unit. "You've heard of the Green Berets?" I imagined myself saying. "Well, Roman is with the Airborne's Red Mohawks."

~

"Don't worry, Mom. I'm going to shave it off at the end of this leave. I'll have to," he said. "It's just that I've always wanted to do something crazy with my hair. And I figured this was my last chance."

I trusted he was looking ahead to his role someday as a responsible post-Army adult. But like the dark smoke of a roadside bomb, the idea of "lasts" hovered over that ten-day leave, colored it in ways Clairol never thought of. Anyone with someone they love heading into harm's way knows this.

To their credit and his, the sixty-or-so friends and neighbors who came to the block party took Roman's hair in stride. It was a vindication of sorts, if any was even needed. Men slapped him on the back and laughed. Kids said, "Cool." Moms wrapped their arms around him. In spite of differing views about the war, everyone there wished our unconventional soldier well.

I confess I still thought the new, albeit temporary, look of his was not the most mature thing Roman's ever done. And then he surprised me again—with something that was. It came in answer to a question I asked one day after dinner.

We'd been talking about how time flies, and how the end date of his four-year stint in the service would come up while he still had three months left in Iraq.

"Well, then. Think the Army might let you come back sooner?" I asked. "You know, before the rest of your unit?"

Roman shot me a look that said he couldn't believe I was asking that.

"Mom, even if the *Army* would, *I* couldn't do that. Say to my men, 'See ya! I'm outta here!'? No way. No. I'll come home when they do."

It was a moment to remember, one of many from ten days that were too few.

TARGET PRACTICE

JULY 2005

The trip to the shooting range was his idea.

"Come on, Mom. It'll be good practice for me while I'm here at home. You and Dad can try it, too. I'll show you how," Roman said.

Growing up, he'd often heard us say, "Whatever you do, do your best." Earlier that day he'd boasted about his recent scores—highest in his unit—at the rifle range in Fort Campbell.

"Uh, no. Really. Thanks. That's OK." I said, more than a little surprised by his invitation.

I had my reasons for saying no. Several years earlier, a friend's little girl lost her eye in a BB gun accident. A couple years after that, our neighbor across the street—a university professor—was killed, along with two of his colleagues, when a graduate student shot them at San Diego State University.

Not long ago a teenage girl we knew tried to kill herself with the handgun hidden in the quiet suburban home she shared with her mom and dad. She very nearly succeeded.

Toy guns had never been part of Roman's childhood. The shelves in his room had teemed with other things: Legos, plastic dinosaurs, books, Play-Doh, finger paints.

But here he was, with only a few days left of his leave, asking if I'd join him at the shooting range. I think he knew his dad could be counted on to say yes, especially if I were on board with the idea too.

"Come on. It'll be a new experience for you!" His voice was sincere.

It seemed to me there was more to this request than just the promise of a new experience. I think Roman was proud of his achievements on the range and wanted to show off a bit. But in his words I also heard: "This is a big part of my world these days. It's what I do in the service of this country. It might not be a campus tour, but it's the thing right now that's mine to show you."

And I realized, too, that in the months ahead, Roman's very life could depend upon this skill. Like it or not, in war it's a good thing to be good at.

"OK, then," I heard myself answer.

~

"So, which target do you want?" the guy at the American Shooting Center asked, jerking his head toward the line of poster-like papers hanging above the counter. The three of us—Roman, his dad, and I—had agreed we'd share the same gun and target. We'd already signed the center's standard release forms and been issued protective goggles and heavy-duty plastic earmuffs. The guys chose the weapon: a handgun, a 9mm Beretta. And they settled on the number of bullets we'd need: 100.

The target choices ranged from the traditional concentric circles to the image of a broad-shouldered man in silhouette.

"You pick, Mom," Roman said graciously, sensing, I think, how strange I felt there among the for-sale Remingtons, holsters, and "Got Ammo?" baseball caps.

A few minutes later, leaning against the cinder-block back wall of the indoor range, I watched him and his dad work together on taping our target of innocuous geometric shapes to the cardboard on the automated pulley system. With a push of a button, it flew out into our designated shooting lane. And there, 30 feet or so away, jiggling just a little, it waited.

"Want to go first, Dad?" Roman asked after the intermittent gunfire from other shooters in the place had died down. Roman Sr., as new to this as I was, nodded.

The two of them stood side by side behind the barrier between shooters and targets. Almost six inches taller than his dad, Roman had to lean down a bit to show him what to do. Apparently there's much more to it than pointing and shooting. Locks to click. Flanges to slide. Forces to be reckoned with. And Roman explained it all to his father with patience and a professionalism I had never seen in him before.

Over the brassy clink of the empty shells falling on the concrete floor, I heard his heartfelt "Good, Dad. Good!" when one of his father's bullets made a hole near the target's center.

Growing up, Roman had learned from his ever-patient dad how to do many things: tie his shoelaces, toot his saxophone, win at chess, drive a car, work on the engine, mow the lawn, build enclosures for his pets with power tools and pine wood, pedal a mountain bike on rugged terrain, de-bug computer programs. This role-reversal now was something to behold.

Then it was my turn. Roman reviewed all the steps with me several times, slowly, carefully. It seemed, in fact, as if he were more interested in showing his dad and me how to shoot than in showing off what he himself could do.

"You're a natural teacher, you know that?" I said.

"Just part of my job," he shrugged. "Ready?"

Holding the gun with both hands, just the way he'd instructed, I gulped. And in the hesitation that followed, felt his arms fold around me from behind, his cheek rest gently against the side my head, his warm hands encircle my wrists. I stretched my arms forward, his too, closed my eyes, and squeezed the trigger.

Pop!

Amazed by the raw power of the weapon, I recoiled—at the force of the bullet leaving the chamber, but even more so at the realization of the consequences of a force like that. The target trembled, but it was me that was shot through—with an awareness of things most tender and terrible.

ONCE MORE TO THE LAKE

JULY 2005

Roman's leave was winding down. At the start of it, I'd asked him to save the last Saturday afternoon for me. I knew then that his time here at home would be busy. There were friends from his high school days he wanted to have fun with—parties to go to, girls to dance with, movies to see. "All good," as they liked to say.

When I'd asked him to reserve for me the Saturday before he left, I had some quieter Quality Time in mind—an afternoon at Lake Miramar, just the two of us and a rented canoe. It's one of my favorite things to do. And before my son left, I wanted to do it with him.

The lake—a reservoir, actually—is a short drive from our home. Roman and his dad used to ride their mountain bikes from here to the path that follows its meandering shoreline. With the lap of its waves, the quack of its ducks, and the rustle of wind in the tall trees that fringe its marshy edges, Lake Miramar is just about as far from the desert as a person can get.

Roman and Sue Diaz at Lake Miramar in San Diego, California, July 2005.
Photo by Sue Diaz.

For most of the guys in his infantry unit, the impending deployment would be their first in a war zone. But Roman already knew all too well what it feels like to be awakened by the whistle of falling mortars, to hoist a heavy machine gun in the searing heat, to be looking in the rear-view mirror of the Humvee you're riding in and see the one behind you disappear in a fiery flash.

When Roman came home—safe and sound—from his first deployment, I was sure the front-lines chapter of his four-year stint in the Army was over. Then he got these orders, this new assignment.

I didn't even want to think about it.

What I had allowed myself to think about was that our afternoon at Lake Miramar would be special, a chance for me to say things that weren't easy to work into day-to-day conversation. The kind of talk Roman had deflected with embarrassed "Oh, Mom's" pretty much since he turned thirteen.

I anticipated an opportunity to tell him how proud I was of him. How much I've admired the way he's handled all that he has been through in the last three years on this path he knew I never dreamed he'd take. I wanted to remind him how much he is loved. Not just by me and his dad and his sis-

Roman Diaz taking a break in a canoe at Lake Miramar, San Diego, California, July 2005. Photo by Sue Diaz.

ter, but by his grandparents, aunts, uncles, cousins, neighbors, friends, and even people he's never met, a nation that, politics aside, appreciates a soldier's sacrifice.

Roman and I settled into our canoe. He sat at the bow, looking down the length of the narrow boat, the only direction that particular seat allowed. I was in the middle seat, facing him. The dock attendant handed each of us an oar and with his push from the pier, we were launched.

Several yards out, we began paddling, each of us stretching forward a bit to dip an oar into the water and then pull it along opposite sides of the canoe. But something was wrong. We were going nowhere.

We dipped the oars and tried again. Same thing.

"Wait a minute," Roman said. "For this to work, aren't we both supposed to be facing the same way?"

"Oh, yeah," I said, amazed I hadn't noticed it sooner. It was too late. The canoe's inherent wobble, my inherent klutziness, made my pivoting around at that point a little too risky. And he was wedged in at the bow. For one or the other of us, rowing was going to be awkward—a push, not a pull. Gliding at a good clip was out of the question. What could we do but shake our heads and laugh?

Determined, it seemed, to keep things light, my co-captain let out an, "Arggggghhhhhhhh, Matey," like the pirate he was so many Halloweens ago. As we lurched across the lake, he swung his oar every now and then in a ridiculous 360-degree arc: in, through, behind, up, over. I rolled my eyes. Next he teased that we'd sprung a leak. "Man the lifeboats, Mom!" By the time we'd nearly run aground in a shoreline thicket of reeds, all hope for a serious heart-to-heart was gone.

Several pink caviar-like clusters clinging to the stalks of the reeds caught his eye, and he shifted gears a bit. Wondered what they were. Then he plucked a snail off one of those same plants, and holding it in his hand, studied it with the focused curiosity that characterized him as a boy. I fumbled for my camera. He glanced up. I took his photograph. He reached for the slim point-and-shoot in his shirt pocket, smiled, and snapped mine.

We drifted for a while—how long, who can say?—under the warm sun, with a nice breeze and our own thoughts.

"Beautiful day, huh?" I offered at last, as much to the air as to anyone.

"It is," Roman echoed softly. "It is."

~

In the months that followed, when I'd see a group of American infantry-men on patrol in the news in their look-alike desert cammies, I'd often replay that afternoon and other memories from that leave—the trip to the range, the silly hair, the serious conversations—and be reminded of the individuality not just of my son, but of every single soldier in every band of brothers. And I'd think about all that we as a country lose when even one of them falls.

WALKING THE WALK

MID-AUGUST 2005

Through the wavy triple-digit heat of the Mojave in midsummer, the Humvee headed our way up the long sloping road. From the front seat of our parked car, I tracked its progress, stepping outside as it got closer.

"Think that's him?" I asked Roman Sr.

"Hard to tell," he said, peering in the same direction.

It was Saturday, late in the afternoon, at the main entrance to the Army's Fort Irwin, near Barstow, California. Roman was there with his unit for three weeks of desert training. When it was finished, they'd be flying back to Kentucky to prepare for deployment to Iraq next month.

Earlier, just after lunch, he'd called us at home with news that he'd been given the night off. "You guy's wouldn't by any chance have plans to be near Barstow later today, would you? Because if you did, you know, we could maybe get together for dinner or something."

The invitation was vintage Roman. Wry. Low-key. Unassuming. He knew, of course, that we were as likely to be near Barstow as we were to be planning a weekend in Baghdad. But he also guessed his parents would be happy to make the three-hour drive on the spur of the moment for one more chance to see him. He was right.

The plan wasn't without complications. When we arrived at the guard station at the fort's south entrance, the MP there informed us we wouldn't be allowed on base unless we were accompanied by our soldier.

"Wait over there," the guard said pointing to a paved spot nearby. We pulled over. Parked. Rolled down all the windows. Opened the front doors. My husband used his cellphone to call Roman on his.

"Hey, all right! You made it!" Roman answered. "Soon as I can find a ride, I'll be there."

Roman Sr. got out, sighed, stretched, and paced. I unbuckled my seat belt, leaned back, and took in the scene around me: low hills dotted with rocks and scrub, trails etched into the hard, dry terrain. In spite of the small city of boxy buildings a couple miles down the road, and all the cars and trucks passing the guard station on their way out, Fort Irwin seemed to be mostly sky and sand. In a place like that, thoughts have lots of room to wander. Mine did, to Roman—twenty-one and on the brink of going to war for the second time.

No matter how old our children are, it's hard as a parent not to still think of them as kids. And whenever my son had been home on leave, he hadn't gone out of his way to change this view. He'd typically sleep in. Shuffle into the kitchen in bare feet and baggy jeans. Open the refrigerator, idle there for a while, bypass the V8 juice in favor of a can of Pepsi. Schlep to the family room sofa for some channel surfing, happy as can be to rediscover Sponge-Bob SquarePants.

And that was OK. If anyone deserved to be cut some slack, it was a kid who'd been to Iraq and back. And was headed there again.

No longer a lowly private, this next time he'd be in charge of a group of men. Most were older than he, he'd told us. Some married, with children.

I tried to imagine the little boy I used to call "Bunky" barking orders to men carrying machine guns. Tried to picture the laid-back teenager I knew now giving instructions in how to clean a weapon, pack a duffle, carry a wounded comrade. Try as I might, I couldn't do it.

And wondered if I'd ever begin to understand what he's been through and how he's changed; if I'd ever be able to see him, really see him, not so much as my son, but as someone separate from my memories, someone coming into his own in the complicated world beyond our backyard. It would require a fundamental shift in perception. And in those families where this sea change somehow happens, it means, I think, not only that the child has grown up, but that the parent finally has, too.

The Humvee we'd been watching stopped about a block away, just before a turnaround point. I saw the door on its right side swing open, a backpack land on the pavement, a tall soldier in camouflage khakis jump out. I was sure I'd recognize Roman, even from a distance, just by the way he moved. I looked for that ambling walk of his I knew so well.

The manner in which this fellow carried himself was something else entirely. Back straight. Chest out. He'd scooped up his pack with one hand, and with the other gave the hood of the Humvee an authoritative thump, then pointed as if giving directions. With a quick, full-arm wave to the guys inside, he turned and headed up the road toward us and the guard station. His stride, smooth and sure.

I shrugged. Not him.

I turned to get back into the car, when somebody called out. "Hey, Mom! Dad!" I heard him say, in a voice familiar as my own.

HURRICANE KATRINA

EARLY SEPTEMBER 2005

For a while at least, Hurricane Katrina made Iraq go away. Or so it seemed. I should know. I'd been a news junkie when it came to the Middle East.

Even after Roman and the 1st Armored Division came home, I continued to follow events in Iraq closely, reading each day the news from that beleaguered country. *Union-Tribune* stories of ignored experts, gross miscalculations, botched security, suicide bombs, bungled aid, porous borders, angry Iraqis, an invigorated insurgency, and an American president who insisted on "staying the course" for reasons that shifted over time from national security and WMDs to polling places and purple fingertips—and all to the tune of hundreds of billions of taxpayer dollars. Stories of Hurricane Katrina blew off the front page at the end of summer in 2005.

Many evenings before Katrina happened, I watched the segment of the CBS News called "The Fallen," a two-minute profile of yet another American the war had claimed, complete with snapshots of that individual in happier times.

Katrina changed that, too. For a time, photos of children separated from their families in the hurricane's aftermath replaced those of soldiers in a CBS News segment called "The Lost."

In the days right after the hurricane, when the rooftops of New Orleans were dotted with the desperate, and the Superdome teemed with people and misery, I watched, stunned and helpless, like all Americans, as the levees broke and the floodwaters rose. Watched and waited for help to arrive, for the most prosperous country in the world to come to the aid of its own. Watched and waited.

The devastation from Hurricane Katrina was worse than anything terrorists anywhere had ever wrought. Nature, not FEMA's Michael Brown, had done "a heck of job." In the years since September 11, 2001, our government and its resources had been focused "like a laser," the President had said, on protecting us from the terrorists. But our leaders had largely ignored the warnings of what we could do, by omission, to ourselves. The levees around New Orleans were, literally, a disaster waiting to happen. A disaster that would leave its mark, not on sixteen acres of midtown Manhattan, but across thousands of square miles of America.

And when it did, we appeared to have neither the wherewithal nor the focus to respond as we should have. New Orleans descended into chaos. And while people there languished on its curbs and died of dehydration, their Louisiana National Guard was on the other side of the earth, patrolling the streets of Iraq.

Images of federal help—troops—finally arriving in New Orleans were still fresh in my mind when, sitting at my computer, I saw the icon pop up that told me Roman was online back in his barracks at Fort Campbell.

Our conversation started as it always does.

Hey there! How goes it? I typed.

It goes.

After a few lines of chit-chat about the sandwich he was eating, his dad's new job, and his own plans for the weekend, we moved on to bigger things.

Was there ever any talk there of the 101st going to Louisiana instead of Iraq? You know, to help with hurricane relief? I asked.

No. I wish though. I'd like that. It would almost be like the reverse of Iraq.

Water, water everywhere? I said, stating the obvious. But that's not what Roman meant. And the next words, coming from a young man who prided himself on being a good soldier, hit me with the force of a Gulf Coast hurricane.

No. Instead of shooting people, we'd be helping.

How do I respond to that, I wondered. How does any American in this fear-filled post-9/11 world respond to that? I thought for a minute, then typed,

That would be a welcome change, huh?

Roman's answer came back in a heartbeat:

Yes.

SARGE

MID-SEPTEMBER 2005

I didn't need to read between the lines there on my computer screen in the MSN Messenger dialogue box. The meaning of Roman's Instant Message was clear. He was worried. Worried he might not pass the test that would mean his promotion from specialist to sergeant.

"Just do your best," I tapped out on my keyboard. "And you'll do fine."

But he didn't see it as that simple, and he proceeded to tell me why. He'd been given a practice test that morning, and he blew it, he said, big time. With the real test less than 24 hours away, he seriously doubted he'd be earning an extra stripe anytime soon.

A bright kid who'd always coasted to good grades, Roman had never been fond of memorizing facts for multiple-choice tests. And that was the kind of test this one was. Specifics. Technical details. Map reading. Procedure following.

"If I don't pass tomorrow," he typed, "I won't be able to try for sergeant again for another six months."

But to his way of thinking, that wasn't the worst of it. If he didn't make sergeant, he wouldn't be allowed to continue leading the group he'd actually been put in charge of training for the past couple of months. His previous boots-on-the-ground experience in places like Baghdad and al-Kut had been, I think, a factor in his being given those responsibilities shortly after he arrived at Fort Campbell, Kentucky, back in January. None of the other men in his new squad had ever been to war. But that's where the 101st would be going in a few weeks. Roman, too, along with the guys he'd nicknamed his "Jedi."

Unlike them, he knew what lay ahead. Knew from experience that being well trained could mean the difference between life and death. Physical fitness, for instance, matters greatly when you've got a fifty-pound pack on your back, a six-foot wall between you and cover, and insurgent bullets churning up the dirt at your feet.

With that knowledge, Roman had taken it upon himself to be an after-hours running coach for one of the soldiers in his group, a hefty guy, whose extra pounds had been slowing him down in their daily physical training. I could easily picture my lanky son showing that young man how to pace himself, how to breathe, and—true to form—lobbing just enough good-natured insults to keep the guy moving and motivated.

"You know, it's kinda weird, but with some of these guys, I almost feel like their dad," he had told me when he was home on leave in July. And if it felt strange for him to say that, it felt even stranger for me to hear it.

Whenever he spoke of his soldiers, I heard something else in his voice as well. A certain pride. A growing confidence. A gritty love. The lay-down-your-life kind. It made me proud.

It scared me, too.

As a parent, what I cared most about was him. Not politics. Not history. Not some so-called noble cause. I would have agreed, in principle, that there are things in this world worth fighting and dying for. But whether or not Iraq was one of them was certainly debatable. What really mattered to this mother, and to others with sons and daughters over there, was that our kids would return home—safe, sound, whole. The feeling was as powerful as it was instinctual. Ideology paled in comparison. Democracy in the Middle East? Or, dancing someday at your child's wedding? In my heart, it was no contest.

So when Roman typed that he might not make sergeant, a selfish hope stirred. I already knew that his four years in the Army will be up several months before his division was scheduled to return to the States. But he had already told me that if he was a team leader, he would stay with his guys until they all came home together. My thinking was, if he's not their leader, their sergeant, their "dad," if he's just another "grunt," it might actually be possible for him to leave the war zone sooner.

On the one hand, I wanted him to succeed, to do his best. Of course I did. On the other hand, I also knew that his becoming a sergeant would probably mean more months in harm's way. More bullets to dodge. More waiting roadside bombs to wonder about.

The day of his formal test to become a sergeant, he came online again and typed, "Hey, Mom. I passed!"

I stared at his words and gulped. "Way to go, Sarge!!!" I finally tapped out, adding one exclamation point, then another, and another, hoping those keystrokes conveyed the elation that—forgive me—I could not feel.

THE SPONGEBOB LETTERS
V

October 26, 2005

Hey Dude!

SpongeBob here, your little ol' turtle. Or maybe I shouldn't say "little." I've been growing like crazy. (What else is new, huh?) Have a new trick to prove it. Remember how when I'd want to look over the edge of my enclosure, I'd try to kind of climb up and over and get a peek that way? Well, now all I have to do is stretch my neck. Really. That's all it takes to see the sights on the other side: peach-colored carpet and tangled computer wires, far as my bulge-y eyes can see.

I wish *you* were on the other side. I was so bummed when I heard that you were going back to Iraq—and, to make matters worse, without me! I know, I know, there just wasn't room in your duffle for a tortoise. And supplying me with piles of fresh lettuce everyday once we got there would have been a problem, unless there are special government-issue MREs for those of us of the amphibian persuasion. But lettuce or not, I still wish I was there with you. You could count on me to hiss at insurgents. I'd figure out some way to help democracy get a foothold in the Middle East. And, man, what I'd give right now for a good sandstorm!

Well, I'm counting the days until you and I can hang out together again—sittin' in the grass somewhere, maybe knockin' back a Heineken or two, listenin' to our iPods, checkin' out the chicks. Good times, my friend. Good times.

Get this. Your dad talks to me sometimes. Calls me "Sponger." I don't mind. I know he'd really rather be talking to you. I'm just a substitute in-a-shell. But I do what I can to keep the old people smilin'.

If I stretch my neck a lot I can see some of the Halloween decorations the neighbors next door have put up again this year. Their yard's full of ghouls and bats and skeletons and witches, and Halloween's still a week away! The guy really gets into it. I think at heart he's really still a kid, but has pretty much perfected his day-to-day disguise as a grown-up.

Well, Bro, gotta go. Gonna do some PT (including lots of stretches). Tell those guys you're in charge of that I wish I could trade places with them. I'd follow you anywhere.

Peace out—

SpongeBob

Part Three:
THE HELL OF WAR

LETTERS

In this brown leather box packed with papers from Roman's four years of soldiering, there are only eight letters from him of the old-fashioned hand-written kind. Six from his weeks in basic training, and only two—one per deployment—from Iraq, each of which we'd wryly refer to as "The Letter." If it hadn't been for the Internet, there might be more of those. Then again, maybe not. Communication of any kind with home all but stopped as he and his platoon marched deeper into the thing called war.

I pull out the letter postmarked November 2005 from his second deployment. Back when it arrived, we hadn't heard a word from him for nearly a month—nothing, not an e-mail, not a call.

Now I unfold two pages filled with his unmistakable, mostly all-caps penmanship, and study his sketch near the middle of the first page. It looks like him, in a cartoonish kind of way, though the face is longer. The jaw line, more defined. The eyes, a whole lot rounder. But the peace sign in one hand and the 12-gauge in the other captures his complex character perfectly.

In the letter he told us that his camera had broken, and he wrote, "In the absence of photos, I've included this drawing of myself." He went on to bring to our attention the, as he called it, "ridiculous" Zorro-like mustache he'd added—just barely—in real life and there in the drawing. Said it had earned him the nickname, "Dirty D." In those lines, I heard his laugh. I remember how I felt when I read them for the first time: almost giddy with relief.

The feeling didn't last long. It never did. How could it when every morning, reading the paper with my Cheerios and coffee, I'd turn to the section titled, "Army Deaths," a matter-of-fact listing of who and where. Why did I do this? Hope, I think. Hope that in the not-too-distant future there would be no more names to report, nothing to read under a heading like that. I looked for that feature each morning, hoping never to find it again.

But in the autumn of 2005, there was little chance of that. One morning I remember in particular, that listing was the reason my workday got off to a late start. After seeing four names followed by the letters and numbers I recognized as part of my son's address—502nd Infantry Regiment, 2nd Brigade Combat Team, 101st Airborne Division—I stared for too long out the break-

Self-portrait by Roman Diaz, sent in a letter from Iraq, fall 2005.

fast nook window. I sat there wondering if Roman knew Sgt. 1st Class Jonathan Tesser, Spc. William J. Byler, Pvt. Adam R. Johnson, Pfc. David J. Martin. Wondered if he had been on or near that road south of Baghdad when, as the paper said, "an explosive detonated near their vehicle."

It wasn't out of the question. In an online conversation several weeks before this letter arrived, he had mentioned that he'd been serving as a gunner, a guard, for a convoy. An interim mission he'd volunteered for, he said, "Because the places they stop along the way—like this one—have Internet! So I can check my e-mail." Not the most comforting words in the world, but not surprising either. Roman had always managed to find his way to a computer. Sometimes it had simply been a matter of walking over to the next tent. So when his messages stopped altogether, my concerns grew.

Thanks to the media, I couldn't help but be aware of the physical dangers that surrounded him—and everyone over there—those days. I was not unaware, either, of the toll a war can take in other ways. The invisible shrapnel that tears up souls, lodges in memories, hardens hearts, wounding in ways no one there can see nor the rest of us really understand. The kind of wounds that might, I imagined, cause a soldier to retreat for a time from family, friends, and things once familiar.

Thoughts like those made letter-writing hard—from this side, for sure. I puzzled at times over what newsy news to share, wondering under what circumstances Roman might read the words I'd write. Through what new filter would he view my latest ramblings about Charger games, hassles with work, dinners with friends, visits with his sister and her husband, SpongeBob's latest growth spurts, plays at the Old Globe. I even wondered whether heartfelt "stay safe's" and "we're proud of you's" could, in the midst of war's worst-case scenarios, come to sound like so much "yadda, yadda."

It occurred to me then that news from home might not always be welcome, underscoring as it inevitably would, the differences between peace and war, the "then" and the "now." Not all that long ago, it seemed, I was tucking permission slips for Cub Scout field trips into his pockets, sending him on his way with reminders to "have fun" and "be good." Now as a sergeant he filled the pockets of his khakis with things like extra ammo and just-in-case tourniquets. When he was a boy, he marched off to school with my peanut butter sandwiches in his backpack. That November, it was Uncle Sam's MREs (Meal, Ready-to-Eat). How could a young man reconcile such disparate realities, especially against a backdrop of roadside bombs and memories of buddies who never came back?

The letter offered some assurance that Roman's lack of communication that autumn had nothing to do with any of that. The reason, he said, was logistical and linked to his unit's new long-term assignment.

"My platoon lives way out by ourselves," he explained in the letter, penned by flashlight nearly three weeks earlier. "There is no phone or Internet access in sight. I sleep in a basement. Our food and water is dropped off by Blackhawk helicopter."

The feeling is bittersweet as I read his postscript again: "P.S. If you send a box, please include some peanut butter."

A LETTER FROM HOME
ROMAN NEARLY NEVER READ

December 17, 2005

Dear Roman,

It's a Saturday afternoon. Your dad is mowing the lawn. There's some slow jazz coming from the stereo in the family room, the kind your grandfather and grandmother used to dance to after World War II. I just got back a little while ago from a quick trip to the hardware store, the one in the Vons shopping center. We needed a new fuse for one of the strings of little lights on the Christmas tree. After we got the darn thing up, ornaments, lights, angel—the works—one of the strands went out. So the bottom half was lit and the top wasn't. Which seems kind of fitting this Christmas.

By the time you get this letter, Christmas will be past. Maybe New Year's, too. Let's look ahead to 2006. Let's count on it being a good year. You'll be back from Iraq. That in itself will make it a *very* good year.

We've been watching the news this week for news about the elections over there. Looks like they went pretty well. Lots of Sunnis participated, and that has to be a good thing. Maybe the violence will subside, now that there are other ways—like elections—to gain power. Did your unit play a role in the election process? You know, like providing backup for the Iraqi forces at the polling places? Truly, Roman, you are at forefront of history. I'm sure many times you'd rather be someplace else, anyplace else. But there you are—an eyewitness to huge sociopolitical change. Not just a witness, but a participant. And a leader, too. I admire you for that.

Tonight we might go to a Christmas pageant sort of thing at this church in Rancho Santa Fe. Your dad's boss has a role in it. Rumor has it, the guy is playing the part of Jesus! I'm a little confused, since it seems to me that in a Christmas pageant that role would call for someone considerably younger, like, say, newborn-to-six-months. Hard to picture the vice president of the company, George is his name, in swaddling clothes. (Can't say that I want to, either.)

I'm hoping we'll hear your voice sometime over the holidays. Hope that you'll be able to get to a phone—or that the Army will get a phone to where you guys are.

Let's see, what else? We rented the movie *March of the Penguins* last night. It's a documentary that created quite a buzz, kind of like *Fahrenheit 9/11*, though the topic it explores is more cute than controversial. Penguins, no matter what they are doing, are cute. And these were walking—trundling—more than 70 miles to find their mates. How cute is that?

Speaking of cute, SpongeBob continues to charm us with his adorable antics—sleeping, eating, and . . . oh, yeah, sometimes moving—ever so slowly—from Point A to Point B. Though I think the main reason we like him has a lot to do with the young man who first brought him to us. Well, guess I'll close for now.

Take care. Stay safe.

Love,

Mom

DOORBELL MOMENT

One evening not long after that rare letter from Roman arrived, the front doorbell rang unexpectedly. Just two months into the deployment, and already families of four of his comrades had opened their doors to see two soldiers waiting there in dress uniform. It is the sight every parent of a soldier-at-war dreads. And it begins with the sound of a doorbell.

In the thirty seconds or so it took me to reach the foyer after ours rang, I prayed a thousand prayers. It took every bit of strength I had—it always did in those instances—to pull aside the thin curtain of the window-by-the-door. As I did, my fingertips caught the edges of the Blue Star banner that hung there, too.

It had been a hand-sewn gift from my friend, Mary, not long after we'd learned that Roman would be going back to Iraq. The banner's history, Mary told me, dated back to World War I. In that world war and the one after it, she said, most Americans knew that a Blue Star in the window meant someone from that home was serving in the war. A Gold Star told the world that a member of that family had died in service to our country.

Pulling aside the banner, I held my breath and looked out.

"Good evening, Ma'am," a young man said. He was wearing a uniform, but not the kind I'd been dreading seeing. His was a white polo shirt with the logo of a pest-control business on its breast pocket.

I felt relieved, enormously relieved, but that emotion couldn't overcome a much stronger feeling. Fear still filled me when I opened the door and heard him launch into his sales pitch. When he asked if we had an ant problem, he seemed startled by the clenched-teeth intensity of my, "No. No, we don't." Before he could say more, I was already closing the door. "Sorry. Not interested," I choked, even as I could feel the color returning to my cheeks.

"What's *her* problem?" he no doubt thought as he carried his clipboard to the house next door.

Too young to realize the significance of the Blue Star banner, he couldn't have known that my son, who was just about his age, was serving in Iraq. Roman and his buddies might have said that their job, like that guy's, was to rid neighborhoods of unwanted pests. Though in their case, it was insurgents.

I didn't mean to be rude to that young man that evening. Just as I didn't mean to be rude on other occasions to unexpected front-porch callers: neighbors, Girl Scouts, and more than a few Jehovah's Witnesses.

But every Blue Star mother knows, civility, empathy—none of that comes easy when something in you dies every time the doorbell rings.

CHRISTMAS CARD, 2005

Hope this card finds you filled with the season's peace and joy, or at the very least, some angel-shaped sugar cookies.

This year has brought its share of changes and milestones. I'd like to say that Roman Sr. was recently crowned King of the Biotech Software Industry and that I won the Nobel Prize for 850-word essays. Truth is, our workdays—his at a local software company and mine here at my computer—simply continue to keep us both on our toes and happy to do our bit in this world.

Anne married her college sweetheart, Erick, on a Saturday in April that was a beautiful, beautiful day in spite of the rain that almost fell. They'd moved up the date of the wedding so that young Roman (now Sergeant Diaz) could be there. He had received orders earlier to return to Iraq with the 101st Airborne Division, and that's where he is now. But at Anne and Erick's reception and in full dress uniform, he proved that it is indeed possible to dance up a storm in combat boots.

In the ups and downs of our days, we are truly grateful for the people— friends, relatives, colleagues—in our lives. We're grateful, too, for the annual opportunity to have some fun with PhotoShop, but more than that, to wish you and yours a blessed holiday and a happy new year.

Peace,
Sue and Roman Sr.

A CHRISTMAS APART

DECEMBER 2005

I kept hoping we'd be able to talk with Roman on Christmas day. I already knew there was no chance that we'd see him. No chance that that morning he'd be sitting on the sofa near the Christmas tree, munching a three-pound slice of our family's infamous fruitcake. No chance that he'd be there to open gifts or pass them to his dad and me or his sister and her husband.

Judging from his recent letter, odds of a phone call were pretty slim, too. If Roman was able to call, I was hoping it wouldn't be while we were on the road to the annual gathering at his Grandma and Grandpa's. We had missed some of his calls during the first deployment, and I knew what that felt like. We'd come home to find the answering machine blinking, press "Play," and hear messages like: "Hey, Mom and Dad! You there? It's me, Roman. Just callin' to say hi. See how you guys are doin'. Let you know I'm OK."

I could never bring myself to hit the "Delete" button. And so those missed messages from him stayed on the tape. Filled it up over time. While he was in Iraq initially, our answering machine's message-counter never returned to the number "0."

I'd often replay those messages, listening with a mother's ear for what they might tell me about how he was really feeling.

Whenever his voice sounded subdued, I'd worry more than usual. Or smile when I'd catch once again the teasing irreverence of his teen years in a message like this one: "Hi, Old People! It's me, yo' Baby Boy!"

Walking past the piano in the living room a few days before Christmas, I let my eyes fall on another baby boy, the one in the manger scene we display every holiday season. We set it up each year atop the upright piano soon after Thanksgiving, all except the baby Jesus figure, which traditionally I hide in the silverware drawer, or in the china cabinet behind the margarita glasses. On Christmas Eve, either Roman or his sister, in alternating years, had the honor of placing in the manger the baby boy who got this whole holiday started. The Reason for the Season, as they say. The Prince of Peace, whose clear and simple message has gotten lost so often throughout history.

"There is no peace today," I thought, especially there in the Cradle of Civilization, where two millennia ago, legend had it, a light in the east guided three wise men through desert storms and star-filled nights to the makeshift cradle of a little boy. The child who came to change everything, millions believe; though much, it seems, remains the same.

The waiting continues, as it has for thousands of years, for conflicts to end, for hearts to change, for soldiers to come home. Yet every year at this time, hope is also renewed, because if the Christmas story teaches anything, it's that love makes all things possible.

The desert terrain Sergeant Diaz and his squad patrolled might very well have been the same patch of earth traversed by those ancient seekers following a star. And the Middle Eastern sky the three kings gazed into with such hope could easily have been the same one Roman looked up at, when he and his men kept watch by night, though it was crisscrossed with tracer fire and lit up by the blasts of bombs.

This year it would have been Roman's turn to place the boy in the manger. We decided to save that moment for him, to leave the nativity scene on the piano for as long as it might take, until at last he was home for good.

So close to the manger Roman was at Christmas in 2005, and yet, like all of us, so far.

ENCOUNTER WITH AN IED

DECEMBER 23, 2005

"Is this Susan Diaz?" a man's voice said when I answered the phone in my home office. I'd just finished feeding SpongeBob in the bedroom down the hall.

The voice on the other end sounded like a telemarketer. I replied with a wary, "Y-y-e-ss. This is Susan Diaz."

"Is your husband there?"

"He's not available at the moment," I said, rather than offer that he'd left for work an hour earlier and that I was home alone.

The man, all business, introduced himself—Captain Candrian, 101st Airborne—then went on to say that our son had "sustained injuries caused by an IED."

I sat down. Slowly.

"That's an 'improvised explosive device,' Ma'am."

No need for that extra bit of information. Those three letters had become as familiar as PTA used to be.

Above the thumping of my heart I heard Captain Candrian relate details of what he called "the incident." I switched the phone to my left hand, reached for the yellow legal pad I always keep handy, fumbled for a pen, and wrote down these words: Perforated eardrum. Peppered face. Treated at the aid station at Al-Mahmudiyah.

"Could you spell that, please?" I heard myself say. In everyday circumstances, I can be as ditzy as anyone. Ask my husband how many times he's heard, "Seen my glasses anywhere?" But in this situation, my mind was surprisingly focused, almost as if spelling the aid station's name correctly could somehow make right the rest of the story Captain Candrian was telling me.

"Does this mean Roman will get to come home?" I asked, hoping.

"No, Ma'am. His injuries are listed here as 'not serious.'"

I wrote down "NOT SERIOUSLY INJURED" in big block letters. I underlined those words three times and drew a box around them.

"Your son should be back with his unit soon. But you might not hear from him for a few days, because of the, uh, news blackout over there."

He rushed through the last part of that sentence.

"News blackout? What do you mean?"

The captain explained—reluctantly—that when soldiers from a unit have been killed, no one from that group is allowed to phone or e-mail until the next of kin have been notified.

"Oh," I murmured as that sunk in. "Some soldiers died in the attack?"

"Yes, Ma'am."

"Do you know their names?"

"Yes, Ma'am. But I can't tell you that."

I thought about the almost paternal affection I'd heard in Roman's voice during his last leave when he had talked about the guys in his fire team. In the months at Fort Campbell before being deployed, he'd shared dinner at the homes of some of them, played cards with their parents, met their wives, high-fived their kids.

"It's up to me now to make sure they all come home," Roman had said of the men he'd been assigned to lead.

The day after Captain Candrian's call we learned from the newspaper that the attack claimed two soldiers: Spc. William Lopez-Feliciano and platoon leader, 1st Lt. Benjamin T. Britt.

The news blackout from within the unit ended on Christmas Eve with this e-mail from Roman.

"Just wanted to send you guys a quick note and wish you Merry Christmas," he wrote. "I love you both so much and rarely get a chance to tell you these days. I really wish I could be back there to celebrate with you. If I concentrate real hard I can almost taste the shrimp you cook every year, Mom, even though it isn't my favorite."

I smiled at the wise-guy honesty of that last statement. It was so Roman.

He signed off with "Sgt. Diaz" and added this: "P.S. If you guys make it to church, say a prayer for the men of Bravo Company. It's been a rough deployment so far. Any prayers are appreciated."

That was it. No mention of "the incident." Not a word about his injuries. And a telling silence on the subject of the fallen.

He doesn't know we know, I realized.

The next day—Christmas Day—we talked with him on the phone. "I can't believe they did that!" he said when he heard—with his good ear—that the Army had called us. As far as he was concerned, the less said, the better. It was a matter of protection, I think. Ours certainly. And maybe his own.

Roman was learning much about life the hard way. But it seemed to me that there was something he didn't as yet completely comprehend or perhaps had come to understand far too well. It was this: When he and his men are out on a mission, they are not alone. Whether we agree with this war or not, those of us who love them are out there, too—moms and dads, kids and cousins, sisters and brothers, neighbors and friends.

Every time an insurgent bomb blows apart a Humvee or a squad on foot patrol, the shock waves from the blast reverberate in small towns like Wheeler, Texas, and big cities like San Diego. A young private takes a bullet; back at home his father's heart bleeds. A soldier loses a leg; his wife struggles in the days that follow to simply keep putting one foot in front of the other. A sergeant's eardrum is perforated; his mother hears the explosion in her dreams, time and time again. Truth is, the casualties of war go far beyond the numbers from the Pentagon. Love leaves us no choice.

In an e-mail a few days later Roman wrote, "I'm fine, functioning, and back at work with my men. Right where I belong."

"We are there too, Sergeant Diaz. We are there, too," I wanted to tell him, but wasn't sure just then it was something he could bear to hear.

A SOLDIER'S SILENCE

U.S. Deaths in Iraq in 2005: 840   Total since the war began: 2,171
Wounded in 2005: 5,589   Total since the war began: 15,985[15]

MARCH 2006

"So, what do you hear from Roman?" Mary asked, as friends and family often did. My answer was always the same. "Not much," I'd tell them, with a shake of my head and a helpless shrug. "Since that day in December, not much."

That's not the way it was during Roman's previous deployment. Old-fashioned letter-writing had never been his thing, but the first time he was in Iraq, Roman Sr. and I "chatted" often with him online via instant messaging, sometimes for hours at a stretch. We joked that Roman talked to us more in the months he was in Baghdad than he did all through high school.

During those online conversations Roman schooled me then in the shorthand of that new form of real-time communication. "BRB" for "be right back." The letters "OIC" for "Oh, I see." That phrase became a favorite of ours, typed in response to questions about everything from the weather in Baghdad to, occasionally, the political climate—there and here. Our conversations, for the most part though, were chatty and light.

That's not to say Roman's initial fifteen months in the Sunni Triangle were easy. No one's time in Iraq is easy—not by a long shot. But in light of "that day in December" and the region's escalating violence and instability, Roman's first deployment was beginning to look like a march in the park.

I continued to drop a card or a letter in the mail to him a couple times a week, along with an occasional care package. But the only communication we had had from his end in the months since Christmas had been a brief phone call with a bad connection, two short e-mails (one about his bank statement), and a late-night conversation with his dad on Instant Messenger. My husband initiated it when he noticed on his computer screen that Roman had signed in online.

"Is that you, Roman?" he typed, clicked, then waited for an answer.

Finally it came. "Hey! What's up, Pops!"

"How are you, Roman?"

"Eh, I'm alright. How are you?"

Their "hellos" behind them, a few lines later my husband asked, "Do you want or need anything from over here?"

"No, I'm good."

"How about some *chicharrones* or pickled pigs feet?" (Convinced, apparently, that the way to a soldier's heart is through an eclectic assortment of pork-based snack foods.)

"No, really, Dad. I'm good."

"Need any extra armor?"

"No."

"Jackets?"

"No. It's going to warm up soon."

And so it went. A fatherly offer here, a quick "no" there. Interspersed with small bits of small talk about the Olympics, rumors of a recent troop visit by Jessica Simpson, and at the end, a sudden, "Dad, I gotta go."

The next morning my husband shared with me their conversation, and coupled with Roman's silence in recent months, the gist of it all seemed to me to be, "Mom, Dad. For your sake and for mine right now, don't love me so much."

I didn't really understand what his reticence meant, but I wanted to try. The Web was as good a place as any to begin. On one site I read about the psychological aspects of combat. It described "psychic numbing as a defense mechanism and an aid to survival for the soldier." Another noted, "If troops think too much about emotional issues in combat situations, it could undermine their effectiveness in battle."

I closed my eyes and saw my son's face. He didn't return my gaze. Of course not. How could he, when he stared down death every day he was over there? I pictured him heading out on another mission, no glance backwards, at me, or anyone or anything he loves, or wants. There was nothing, nothing I could do, but whisper a prayer that he would come back.

Lt. Col. Jerry Powell, an Army chaplain for eighteen years, veteran of Iraq, and cyber-friend of mine, explained something else. "Soldiers do not have the ability to describe the events because the activity is so visceral," he told me in an e-mail. "They are able to share the experiences with one another only by looks, tears, hugs, and the inevitable Army grunt. To convey the same emotions and thoughts to parents is just not possible. The only alternative is silence.

"When I called home during my deployment," Lieutenant Colonel Powell continued, "the sound of my wife's voice on the other end caused such a lump in my throat I could not speak for a moment. I could only squeak out, 'Hi' and let her talk until I composed myself. I blamed the phone connection when she asked if I was there and could I hear her, when the real problem was I was wrecked by a simple, 'Hello.'"

And as for what we here at home could do, Powell offered this, "I think that sending funny cards is very healing. Comedy DVDs are a good idea as well. All the squad has seen are all the war movies ever made. What they prob-ably need is laughter late at night when the world goes quiet."

Later, still turning over in my mind the chaplain's words, I recalled the instant messaging phrase Roman taught me back when conversation between us came easier and more often. "OIC," I heard myself sigh, scanning the sale bins at Blockbuster for *Ferris Bueller's Day Off*.

WAR AS IT HAPPENS

For all the emotion in his voice, John Crawford could have been talking about brushing toast crumbs off a breakfast table. Instead, he was telling his audience how, after his unit had been involved in an intense firefight one morning while on patrol in Iraq, he sat down later to an MRE lunch, and, out of the corner of his eye, noticed a small fragment of a man's brains stuck to the side of his boot.

"I flicked it off with the back of my spoon, then went on eating," he said flatly.

I'd been channel surfing from the couch in the family room, and initially it was Crawford's boyish good looks that made me give the remote a rest. I recognized him as the guy on the dust jacket of *The Last True Story I'll Ever Tell: An Accidental Soldier's Account of the War in Iraq*. I'd bought the book last year around the time Roman got his orders for a second tour of duty in Iraq. It had been sitting on my nightstand ever since.

Crawford, who'd served with the Florida National Guard, was speaking at a local Festival of Books, and the event was being broadcast on a cable station. I listened and watched as the camera moved from Crawford's face to the faces of the people who had come to hear him. Some winced at his MRE story. A few closed their eyes. Others slowly shook their heads. I shuddered.

The reason he'd shared that particular anecdote, Crawford explained ear-nestly, was to illustrate how war has its own reality, a reality utterly removed from the one the rest of us know. He went on to underscore that point by recounting a phone call to his wife the day of the boot incident. Early in that conversation, she'd launched into a complaint about the mess their dog had made on their living room rug again.

"Try cleaning up brains," Crawford blurted.

Silence.

"Tell me about it," she finally answered. And against his better judgment, he did.

"Oh, my God. I didn't know," was all she could say.

"She was right," Crawford continued, "she didn't know. No one did, and that was what made it worse, and better."[16]

Roman didn't tell his dad and me much about his day-to-day life over there. "We've been busy," he'd say. Or, "It's been hot here, in more ways than one."

I'd always believed that honest communication is a good thing, but in the case of this war, I wasn't so sure. It's the first conflict in history that, thanks to phones and the Internet, allows its combatants to say "Call for back-up!" and "Hi, Mom" in almost the same breath. But when frontline soldiers and their families are able to articulate in real time the details of life as they know it, gaps in understanding, it seems, could turn into chasms. That was Crawford's contention. And the clearest—sometimes the only—message that could come through in such exchanges would be this one: "You have *no* idea."

A few days earlier, I'd turned to Google for an update on Roman's battalion, narrowing my search by including the specific numbers and letters associated with his unit, along with phrase "101st Airborne." Here's what that tack turned up on www.mnf-iraq.com, the official website of the multinational force in Iraq:

In a separate incident, a patrol from 1st Bn., 502nd Infantry Regiment, 2nd BCT, 101st Abn. Div., received small arms fire from the Yusafiyah power plant south of Baghdad. As soldiers waited for permission to enter the power plant, a van approached and opened fire on the patrol. In the ensuing gun battle two terrorists were killed.

"How goes it?" I later asked my son via Instant Messenger.

He answered as he always did: "It goes," he said. "It goes."

I wanted to know more. Longed to say more. But to be honest, I feared that when all was said and done, neither Roman nor I would know how to reconcile the past and the present: my memories of him as a boy nursing injured birds back to health in blanket-lined shoeboxes vs. images now of a man, a soldier, who in the line of duty had very possibly killed other mothers' sons. Knowledge is power, certainly, but it can be many other things, as well. And maybe that explains why, though I'd bought Crawford's book weeks earlier, I hadn't gotten past the back-cover blurbs telling of a story "savage" and "true."

UP IN SMOKE

Incident at Haditha (March 19, 2006): *Time* magazine reports the first public account of survivors' allegations that Marines ran amok after the death of Terrazas (a fellow Marine). Iraqi human-rights group issues the video of residents describing the rampage. U.S. military confirms accounts by doctors that all the civilians were shot, not killed by a bomb. Witnesses say the dead were in three houses and a car.[17]

MARCH 2006

"Freedom's just another word for nothing left to lose," Janis Joplin sang back in the early '70s. And if those words to "Me and Bobby McGee" were still true, then the soldiers of my son's unit had become some of the freest men on earth. Because just before sunrise on February 5 in Yusufiyah, Iraq, they lost everything.

A fire sparked by faulty wiring roared through the old potato factory twenty-five miles south of Baghdad that had been serving as the forward operating base for Roman and some 120 of his fellow soldiers.

It was the place where, at the end of their day, they'd lay down their weapons, hang up their Kevlar, tug off their boots, and stretch out on their cots. It was where they'd relax, as much as anyone in that part of the world was able to then, and reread letters from their wives or girlfriends, flip through back issues of *Sports Illustrated*, listen to MP3s of 50 Cent or Toby Keith, and munch on care-package cookies baked in kitchens they could only remember.

My husband and I learned about the fire weeks after it happened, not from Roman, but from the newsletter the 101st Airborne routinely sends to its soldiers' families every few months.

"Soldiers at Yusafiyah see it all go up in smoke," the story's headline read.

"It was shortly before dawn when 2nd Lt. David Halpern woke up and realized his forward operating base was burning down," the article continued. I learned that some of the men were away on missions, but most were asleep. Awakened by shouts of "Fire" and the sight of flames as high as the ceiling, they got out as fast as they could, saving their lives, not their footlockers.

Huddled outside in whatever passes for pj's in a war zone, they heard the exploding pop and crackle of the ammunition stored in the building, and saw AT-4 rockets shoot through the burning roof.

"It was like a fireworks show," one of the soldiers was quoted as saying.

No one was injured in the fire, though that group had already known more, much more, than its share of hardship. Since they arrived back in October, six of them had been killed in action, twenty wounded. And even as the blaze turned to smoldering ash, insurgents lobbed six mortars at what was left of the compound.

"The fire could have been devastating for somebody else," their commander, Capt. John Goodwin, said. "But because we've been through so much, we were like 'OK, I guess we'll rebuild and move on.'"

An even stronger resiliency came through in the words of Second Lieutenant Halpern in the story: "It was almost comical. We were like, 'Gee, I wonder what I'm going to write in my journal today—oh, wait, my journal burned up.'"

In my next e-mail to Roman, I asked him about what I had read. He answered that someday he'd tell us those stories himself, but in the meantime, he said, all that we needed to know was that he and his men were fine.

Roman wasn't—and never had been—one to complain, but when his father asked him in an Internet conversation not long after that how things were going, Roman's nothing-if-not-honest reply said it all:

"It varies from week to week, Dad. It's never nice," he typed, and then, doing his twenty-something best to still be reassuring, added, "But sometimes it sucks less."

Next line, true to form, he changed the subject.

Though I never believed the war was justified, I was more than willing to be proven wrong. In fact, I'd hoped I would be. But as the conflict wore on, it became increasingly clear that our leaders had rushed to judgment at the start, connected dots that weren't there, and undermined Iraq's fledgling freedom through egregious errors in post-invasion planning—or the lack of it. Our soldiers were paying the price for those mistakes, as were the good people of Iraq, not to mention America's taxpayers. Hope, that spring, was hard to come by.

"Freedom's just another word for nothing left to lose" was an apt description for the chaos that had become Iraq. And even though I'd opposed the conflict from the beginning, I took no satisfaction, none, in the failures of the administration, nor in the thought that it was "Me and Bobby McGee," not George W. Bush, telling it like it is.

MAKING A DIFFERENCE

When the phone rang shortly before Leno's monologue, I jumped. "Who could be calling this late?" I wondered. It was a relief to hear Anne's voice on the other end.

"I just got an e-mail from Roman!" she chirped. "It made me really happy, so I thought I'd call and share some good news with you."

E-mails from her brother had been rare lately. Even rarer were the words "good news" in connection with the situation over there. Phrases like "civil war" and "ethnic cleansing," words like "Haditha" and "investigation," had darkened hopes that the war would end well, if at all.

"Good news? All right! Tell me," I said, and settled in for what turned out to be one of the best stories this mom has ever heard.

~

A bit of backstory first.

At the beginning of Anne's senior year in high school, she'd asked her dad and me if she could sign up for the post-graduation trip to Europe her English teacher and his wife would be chaperoning. When we'd agreed to let her go, we didn't know then that that spring would bring a letter of acceptance from Stanford University.

We're not poor, but Stanford isn't cheap. With four years of Ivy League tuition looming, Anne's European vacation was starting to look like a real extravagance. She begrudgingly agreed, and the next day asked her English teacher to take her name off the tour-group list.

A few evenings later, the phone rang. It was Anne's teacher, calling to tell us that someone who knew Anne had approached him with an offer to fund her trip, no strings attached. Anonymously.

Turned out there was one small catch, and it came a short time later in the letter that accompanied the check.

"Many years ago," Anne's benefactor wrote, "a good friend of mine gave me a generous gift that made it possible for me to do something I could not afford on my own. She refused to let me pay her back, but instead challenged me to help someone in the future when I was in the position to do so. So this gift comes with 'strings attached.' I pass on to you the challenge to do something special for someone else someday. I promise it will bless you as much, if not more, than the person you help."

~

Fast forward to spring of 2006. With her degree in Urban Studies, Anne was working in the Bay Area as the development and communications manager at a non-profit called BUILD. The purpose of that organization is to motivate high school students from under-resourced communities to start their own businesses. In the process, BUILD's website says, "they become interested in going to college, and they recognize the connection between higher education and a higher quality of life." In the seven years it had been in existence, 100 percent of BUILD's students had been accepted at institutions of higher learning.

College acceptance is one thing; paying for it, Anne knew, quite another. In an e-mail to her dad, brother, and me, she told us about an idea she'd been working on lately:

"I have a request for you. If you were thinking of getting me a gift for my birthday (and you definitely don't have to!!! Honestly!), I would rather that you make a donation to the Glow First-Generation Scholarship Foundation. This fund was set up by a friend and fellow mentor to help some of the students here at BUILD who will be going to college next year but are having a tremendously difficult time paying for it, for a variety of reasons.

"So that you know how committed I am to this personally, I have decided to donate $1,000 to this fund (remember when I was given that trip to Europe my senior year and told I should give back some day? I think this is a great opportunity to do that). I would be honored if you could help me support these students."

It was a moment worth everything, and then some. Anne's brother apparently thought so, too. The night she called us, she recapped Roman's answer to her e-mail. Sergeant Diaz, whose paycheck was probably less than an assistant manager's at a coffeehouse, and whose prized possession was a Chevy S10 pick-up with more than 110,000 miles on it, said he wanted to match his sister's contribution to the fund.

"Put me down for $1,000," Roman wrote in his reply to her e-mail.

Against the backdrop of that spring's gruesome headlines and investigations, the lines between right and wrong, good and bad, seemed to be blurring more than ever. But I still believed the vast majority of our fighting men and women in Iraq were decent human beings, doing an impossible job as best they could in circumstances worse than most of us could have ever imagined. And even as they cursed the heat and counted the days till their tour was over, they longed to know their sacrifices would ultimately make a difference, if not in Baghdad or Basra, then in places back home.

MOONLIGHT AND MIZUNOS

A leg cramp—a doozy of a charley horse—jerked me awake. Sleepless nights were becoming a habit. The numbers of the digital clock near the head of the bed said 3:02. As usual, I was relieved it didn't say 4:44, and the reason for that goes all the way back to 1967.

That summer I was a high-school summer-exchange student in Japan, living in a small city near Nagoya with the Mizunos—father, mother, fifteen-year-old daughter, Noriko, and seventeen-year-old son, Yukio. With deep bows and shy smiles, they'd welcomed me into their home of rice-paper walls and *tatami* floors. And for the six weeks I lived there, they treated me like a member of the family. No matter that less than three decades earlier the brother of my Japanese host-mother had been a kamikaze pilot killed in his attack on an American warship. No matter that a stateside uncle of mine had been decorated for bravery in combat on an island in the Pacific. In my summer of 1967, all of that seemed like ancient history.

The Mizunos spoke little English. I knew next-to-no Japanese. But through sheer determination, elaborate pantomimes, and worn-out phrase books, little by little we managed to communicate. We started out with basics—things like, "Where is the bathroom?" and "What do you like for breakfast?" And one evening in August, moved on to ideas like, "What have we learned from Hiroshima?"

My Japanese father, a doctor, summed up for me his worldview with a simple gesture and a single word. "Peace," he said, placing his hand over his heart.

Throughout that summer, I picked up Japanese words and phrases and grammar rules I still remember. For instance, the word for the number four— *shi*—and the word for death are one and the same. Some people in Japan have such a superstition about this term, they will substitute another word—*yon* —for the number after three.

Since Roman had been back in Iraq, I had this weird notion that if I were to suddenly wake up in the middle of the night, look over at the clock and see "4:44" glowing in the dark, it could only mean one thing. I knew that that made no logical sense whatsoever. But then again, so much else then made even less.

When the war in Iraq first began and phrases like "greeted as liberators" were still being tossed about, I naively believed—wanted to believe—that Roman's time in that country might end up being mainly an interesting intercultural experience, not unlike the one I had my seventeenth summer. I daydreamed that his role would mainly be that of youthful goodwill ambassador. I actually hoped it might be possible that he'd return home with stories of dinner invitations from grateful Iraqi families, new insight into Islam, a taste for cardamom tea or almond cookies, and more Iraqi pen pals than there were people in his platoon.

But my current fear of seeing the clock say "4:44" belied hopes like those and underscored—as much as any headlines—how much things had changed in Iraq since American tanks first rolled into Baghdad.

The shift had been a polar opposite from the change in perception I experienced many summers ago in Japan. For me, that country went from being everything foreign to being four people I came to love. I remember one night after the family was asleep, I tiptoed to the balcony outside my bedroom on the second floor and just sat there, gazing up at the sky. A full moon rose overhead—bright and beautiful. And I was struck by this notion: *Hey that's the exact same moon that shines on Milwaukee! The same moon my mom, dad, sisters, and I look up at from our lawn chairs in the backyard on Elser Avenue!!*

Sitting there with those thoughts and my cotton kimono, I sensed I was on to something. Something obvious, yet elementally profound. I stayed there till my neck was stiff, blown away by the luminous truth of it.

In the middle of another night decades later, I glanced again at the clock—3:04—pushed back the covers, shuffled over to the window, and looked up at the sky. There was that moon again. The same moon that casts shadows from headstones across the graves of the fallen of every nation that has ever gone to war.

Near the start of another summer with Roman in Iraq, that was the new truth that kept me awake.

FROM BAD TO WORSE

JUNE 2006

I was home alone, standing outside on the grass near the corner of the backyard where the kids' Sears swing set used to be, my gaze fixed on the chaparral-covered hills to the east. Above me the sky was clear and blue. A glorious San Diego blue. The kind of sky Shamu does back flips against. But along the upper edges of the hills that fringe our tidy pocket of suburbia, the air was roiling; the sky, changing—darkening there to a gun-metal gray, then deepening to black.

By the time the thought "Brushfire!" formed, a long line of flames had already begun to crest that familiar stretch of hills, less than a quarter mile away.

The wind, hot and dry, kicked up, and soon began to roar. The purple blooms of our flowerbed agapanthas swayed. The climbing roses along the cedar fence trembled. And hummingbirds, moments earlier sipping nectar here and there, zoomed away as fast as their blurry wings could carry them.

But I could not move. This was no ordinary brushfire. And I was transfixed—by its size and the speed with which it was bearing down on the street where we'd lived these past twenty years. I tried to call over the fence to the neighbors, but could make no sound. My mind racing, I willed myself to run inside, gather up family albums and other treasures, jump in the car and take a cue from the hummingbirds.

But try as I might, I couldn't. All I could do was stand there, watching, as the firestorm rushed to claim the home I had loved and the life we had known.

～

Seconds later, my eyes popped open. Instead of standing in the backyard, I was curled on my side in our queen-sized bed, goose-down comforter loosely tucked below my chin and my husband's. I saw the red-glow of the digital numbers—2:44—on the alarm clock near his side of the bed and, over the pounding of my heart, heard his steady breathing.

"It was just a dream," I told myself. "Just a dream. Go back to sleep. There is no fire. Everything's OK. "

But sleep didn't come again that night until I whispered to my husband, "Hold me."

～

It was one of those dreams that stays vivid, even after the dawn. And the next morning, I shared it with the neighbor I walk with every weekday.

"Says something, don't you think, about what's been in the news lately and how you might be feeling about all of that?" Susan said.

I nodded.

"Not to mention Anne's surgery," she added.

For the past year, Anne had been suffering from a bewildering variety of symptoms: high blood pressure, unexplained weight gain, inexplicable bruising, fatigue, anxiety, a new roundness to her face, and an emerging hump on her back. She'd begun losing hair in places where it should be, and started growing it in places where it shouldn't.

She bravely joked that with all of that coming shortly after the wedding, "It was like a fairy tale in reverse." Kissed by a prince, she said, "I'm turning into a toad!" Only it wasn't funny. It was frightening. For months, doctors were stumped. Cardiologists scratched their heads. Endocrinologists said, "Go figure." It took a neurologist to finally connect all the dots and diagnose Cushing's Syndrome, a rare condition that occurs when the body produces high levels of the hormone cortisol over an extended period of time. In Anne's case, the cause was a tumor on her pituitary gland. Brain surgery was scheduled for the first week of July.

Around that same time, word of Roman's battalion and the men of his platoon began reaching us via a string of news stories, gruesome even by

Baghdad standards. The stories were from a place called "Yusufiyah." They arrived like fire in a dream. I wanted to run. But I could not.

ATTACK AT YUSUFIYAH

FRIDAY, JUNE 16

While I was fixing supper, I heard the words "Triangle of Death" in a TV news story telling of an attack on an American patrol at a checkpoint in Yusufiyah—one soldier killed, two kidnapped.

"It's not Roman. It can't be," I told myself. "If it were, you would have known by now."

A friend with more experience as a military mom once convinced me that that's true. Soldiers' families, she said, are notified almost immediately—or at least within a couple hours—after the type of incident that makes the nightly news. So if you're hearing about something for the first time from Bob Schieffer, she had said, you can rest assured that an officer in dress uniform won't be standing on your front porch to tell you the ending of that same story.

Details of the Yusufiyah incident were sketchy throughout the weekend. No names. No particulars, not even a mention of which division the three soldiers were from.

With more than 130,000 American troops in Iraq and the Triangle of Death encompassing an area about the size of Maryland, odds were small, I convinced myself, that Roman or his unit had had any part in the story that was unfolding.

Wanting to be absolutely sure, I Googled several times over the weekend for more information. Entered chains of phrases like "missing soldiers 101st Yusufiyah." But couldn't find anything definitive.

Sunday's *San Diego Union-Tribune* carried a New York Times News Service story that began, "American soldiers on Saturday went house to house, scanned the streets from helicopters and dove into irrigation canals to try to find two of their comrades who had been reported captured by insurgents in an ambush south of the capital." The story later stated, "The apparent capture of the two Americans raises the specter of their public exploitation at the hands of insurgents. Other Americans, including civilian contractors, have been videotaped while they were mistreated, tortured, or killed."

Monday's paper reported, "American forces intensified their search for the two soldiers missing and reportedly held captive by insurgents, widening their pursuit to areas beyond the restive town of Yusufiyah, where the missing servicemen were attacked Friday night, and drawing troops from at least three brigade combat teams."

Still, no names. No specific units.

On Monday on CNN's website, I finally learned the names of all three soldiers involved in Friday's attack—Spc. David J. Babineau, Pfc. Kristian Menchaca, Pfc. Thomas Lowell Tucker—along with the fact that they "were assigned to the First Battalion, 502d Infantry Regiment, Second Brigade, 101st Airborne Division (Air Assault) out of Fort Campbell, Kentucky."

I looked up from the screen of my computer over to a small piece of paper taped to the oak hutch on my desk: Roman's hard-to-remember address. Then back to the screen. Then the paper again. Screen. Paper. Every number and letter on the two, a match.

Just as that was sinking in, a "You've Got Mail" message popped up. It was the e-mail that had just gone out to the families of the soldiers in 502's 2nd Brigade.

"Iraq Communications Blackout," the subject line said.

"In an effort to prevent false or misleading information, the brigade commander has imposed a communications blackout on the 2BCT [2nd Brigade Combat Team] in Iraq. Colonel Ebel understands the emotions many family members may feel based on the recent events in Iraq, and is concerned that false information may cause undue anxiety. Please do not be alarmed by the imposition of this blackout."

Too late for that. I already was. In my mind I replayed the computer-animation I'd seen on CBS of the attack. The streaking gunfire. The three Humvees—one remaining behind at the river's edge, two roaring off in pursuit of the bad guys. Was Roman riding in one of those two vehicles?

The next day, Tuesday, America woke to the news that the missing soldiers had been found, dead, their bodies booby-trapped. Major General Caldwell "said that it was clear the soldiers had died of wounds suffered in captivity, rather than at the site of the attack on the checkpoint, but that the cause could not be immediately determined." The front-page story in the *Union-Tribune* went on to say that Caldwell "declined to describe the condition of the soldiers' bodies. Other officials suggested that the soldiers were so badly wounded or mutilated that they could not be positively identified. The director of the Iraqi Defense Ministry's operation room, Major General Abdul-Aziz Mohammed, said the bodies showed signs of having been tortured. 'With great regret, they were killed in a barbaric way,' he said. He provided no further details. According to residents of Yusufiyah and a relative of one of the victims, the soldiers were beheaded."

As the information blackout from Roman's brigade stayed in effect for several more days, I tried to make some sort of sense of the war story that had hit closer-to-home than most. Exactly how close, I still didn't know. Ignorance wasn't bliss. It was hell. There was some comfort, though, in knowing that sooner or later we would hear our boy's voice once again. Yet my heart ached for those whose sons and brothers had been so brutally silenced.

Sitting at my computer, I clicked again to online photos of the fallen, and took in their oh-so-young faces, their open smiles. And in that instant, I was sitting on a couch in Madras, Oregon; at a kitchen table in Houston; on a front porch in Springfield, Massachusetts; slowly turning the pages of their family photo albums, listening in on memories of Little League games and fishing trips, favorite pets and first cars. All the while trying to understand how prayers are answered, or not, in the Triangle of Death. But understanding didn't come; only tears did, for us all.

FALLEN EAGLES

JUNE 22, 2006

"It is with a heavy heart that I write this this morning, as I am sure the events of the past week are weighing heavily on yours," the wife of Bravo Company's commander said in an e-mail to families of the unit. "I know that most of you are watching the news right now, but I have been told to send this out anyway. The bodies of Menchaca, Tucker, and Babineau

Insignia of the 101st Airborne Division, the "Screaming Eagles." Department of the Army.

have been positively identified by the military. Therefore, the communications blackout has been lifted, and we should begin to hear from our soldiers soon. . . . I am sure we are all freaked out by everything that has happened to B Co, and wondering how the soldiers are doing. Our soldiers are strong, and I know that they have a Combat Stress Team available to help them through this horrific time. Please keep them, and the families of Menchaca, Tucker, and Babineau in your prayers. Thank you for all you do to help this company. Sincerely, Risa Goodwin."

Three days later, Roman contacted us online.

"Hi, Mom," he began his Instant Message.

My heart leapt to see his words on the screen, but my fingers hesitated over the keys. I didn't know what to say, where to begin.

I fell back on our familiar opening lines.

"How goes it with you?"

"It goes," he said. "It goes."

"How are you, what with all that has been happening there?"

"I'm OK."

My fingertips drummed lightly on the keys, not enough to put words up on the screen, but enough to make a soft rattling sound. I stared at the Instant Message box. Rattle. Rattle. Finally the question that needed to be asked pushed its way out, keystroke by keystroke.

"Did you know those three soldiers?"

The computer screen stayed blank. Blank for long seconds. Then Roman's instant-message reply: "Yes."

My fingers froze.

"It bothers me, Mom, that you know so much. I miss the days when I could act as a buffer. Some horrible shit goes on, and people back home don't need to see it, or hear about it, or worse, associate any of it with you."

A few lines later he volunteered this:

"I was supposed to be there (at the checkpoint) with two of my guys. My squad leader didn't feel like changing out and their squad leader (who was my old squad leader) was cool where they were at," he wrote of his team's position relative to the attack.

My breath slowed, then stopped for a moment, as I realized just how close Roman had come to being one of the three.

"I don't know what to say," I typed, adding after another long pause, "I'm just grateful you're OK."

"So what's new with you guys?" Roman countered, shifting the conversation to everyday things: weekend plans, the contents of a recent care package, the "glorious" air-conditioning on base.

What else could he—we—do?

~

In early July another e-mail arrived from the captain's wife. That message told of a link to a website where a short video of the memorial in Iraq for the three could be viewed.

"Families, this is some rough footage of what happens at the memorials in Iraq," she wrote. "I wish we had it in its entirety to share, but I think we can get an idea from it. The beginning starts without sound, so don't fret. Some of it is very emotional. Let's keep all the soldiers in our prayers."

Her request was rooted in the realities of that deployment. Since the approximately 135 men of Bravo Company began their tour of duty back in October, ten had been killed, more than thirty injured seriously enough to be sent home. Others had been routinely patched up at the aid station in Al-Mahmudiyah after run-ins with roadside bombs or bands of insurgents, and then sent back to the unit to fight another day. After their forward operating base—an old potato factory—had burned to the ground in February, I remember thinking, "Things can't get much worse."

I was wrong.

In the weeks immediately following the June attack at Yusufiyah, reports surfaced of more atrocities in the area south of Baghdad. Atrocities allegedly committed not *against* the men of Roman's platoon, but *by* them.

On Saturday, July 1, the *Union-Tribune* reported on its front page, "The U.S. military is investigating accusations that soldiers raped an Iraqi woman in her home and killed her and three family members, including a child, American officials said Friday. . . . The American investigation began June 24, one day after two soldiers 'reported alleged coalition involvement' in the deaths of the Iraqi civilians. . . . American officials, who spoke anonymously because they were not authorized to speak publicly about possible criminal proceedings, said the investigation involved five soldiers from the 502d Infantry Regiment. . . . The alleged rape and killings came to light after a soldier felt compelled to talk about it in a 'counseling-type session,' after the discovery of the bodies of his kidnapped colleagues."

～

I clicked on the link to the video of the memorial service. White letters on a black background told the date and place: June 26, 2006. Al-Mahmudiyah, Iraq.

June 26. Two days *after* one of the unit's soldiers told his superiors what he knew of the rape and murder.

That soldier's allegations set in motion an internal investigation that led to criminal charges against four from the platoon. An investigation that must have already been moving forward when the memorial took place.

It meant the men accused of those crimes couldn't have been among those sitting in the folding chairs that faced the plywood platform at the front of the room.

Three helmets, flanked by flags, perched atop the barrels of three combat weapons, each positioned between a pair of empty boots, each dangling a set of dog tags. The three men, forever young and smiling, gazed out from behind the glass of the framed photos on the wall just behind their helmets.

I could only imagine the depth of the emotions that must have filled the room that day, but the details I observed in the video offered some clue: the seasoned chaplain, both hands gripping the sides of the lectern, faltered over the first words of his speech. Later, a young woman in desert khakis stood in that same spot, closed her eyes, leaned into the microphone, and lifted her voice in and with "Amazing Grace." Her image blurred for a moment as the camera wobbled in the hands of the soldier doing the taping.

Whenever the camera pulled back, I scanned the room for a lanky guy with dark hair and ears that stuck out a little too far. But from the back, they all looked like brothers.

And brothers they were—in the loss of their comrades, in their thoughts about the men under arrest, and in the loss of any innocence they might have still had before the events of the previous week and a half. The memorial made clear there were heroes in their midst. But it seems that earlier there were sinners, too.

The video played on. In a segment near the end, the soldiers heard one of their own read from the Old Testament. As that young man looked up from the text and out at the group, I envisioned his mom, at home, like I was, watching that video. We had never met, but we were sisters, she and I. And her boy was speaking not only to his brothers-in-battle, but also to that larger family every one of us is part of—the family that extends far beyond the familiar faces of those who wait back home, to all who shared in the anguish of these times.

In a voice, strong and steady, he intoned the words from the prophet Isaiah that urged the embattled men of the 101st Airborne—and the rest of us, too—to believe, in spite of everything, in worthier possibilities: to run and not grow weary, to soar on eagles' wings.

LUCINDA, KEEPING IT REAL

G o on, Sue. *Tell them,* Lucinda whispers.
Tell them what?
You know.

No. What?

Tell them about that section in your father's D-Day diary you didn't want to write about.

I . . . uh . . . I don't know what you're talking about.

Well then, let me refresh your memory. It's the entry for September 15, 1944. Your father is writing about leaving Belgium and going to Germany. Kornelimünster, to be exact, the site of his unit's new Command Post. Remember what he wrote about the German people he encountered there?

Uhm . . .

Remember the chill you felt in your soul the first time you read that section? How you couldn't wrap your head around the fact that a man as kind and as good as your father could have written what he wrote? How those words contradicted everything you knew your dad to be? Remember?

All right! All right! Yeah. I do remember. But let's just drop it, OK? He was marching into enemy territory. It was war. And war does things to people, even the best of us.

Indeed it does. That's why I won't drop it. Your father's frankness in that passage reveals a truth that's part of every war story: the capacity for evil exists in us all.

The capacity for good, too! What about that? What about, "Greater love than this no man hath, that he lay down his life for his friend"?

Of course. That's the part of the human heart we're proud to lay claim to. It's the other side, the dark side, we want to deny. It's been said, you know, that "There are no winners in war." If these words from the diary of an American soldier, a decent man in a "good war," don't prove it, then I don't know what does. So, if you won't tell them, Sue, I will.

Fine. Have it your way, Lucinda.

OK then. Here goes. The passage starts out innocently enough, as a straightforward description of the troops' relocation. "We moved about 30 miles from the last Command Post," your father writes. "On the way passed the armor again. The Luftwaffe came out and it was the most German planes I had seen since the invasion. There were about a dozen of them." As your dad travels on, he comes face to face with German civilians, and his tone changes. Remember?

Yes.

I can't hear you.

YES!

Then the gentle man you called "Daddy" continues. "Going through the towns and seeing the German people who appear to be very stunned and bewildered. They're singing a different tune now, the bastards, and some of them even had the nerve to start waving at us. But they won't get any sympathy from me. In fact, almost felt like taking a 'pot shot' at many of them."

"Almost" is the operative word there, Lucinda. He didn't cross that line.

Parse it any way you like. The hate still comes through. And in this case that hatred isn't aimed at enemy combatants, but rather at mothers, fathers, grandparents, and—who knows?—maybe even kid brothers and little sisters, bewildered, waving.

You're a piece of work, you know that? Feel better now? Do you? Now that that's out there?

To tell you the truth, not really.

Guess you could say there are no winners here either, huh?

Roger that, Sue. Roger that.

OPERATION BRAIN SURGERY

JULY 5, 2006

"We should have been able to see Anne by now! What's taking so long!?!" I hissed to my husband as we sat in the waiting room on the main floor of the University of California San Francisco Medical Center. Patient as ever, he patted my knee.

It had been a long day. We'd arrived at the hospital with Anne and Erick just after dawn. Anne had been wheeled into her scheduled surgery at 8:30 and then over to the recovery room, we'd been told, at around 11:00. A nurse had also informed Erick that they'd call down from post-op to let us know when she came out of the anesthesia. Then we could go up to see her and meet with the surgeon.

"Shouldn't be more than a couple hours," the nurse promised.

Now it was nearly three o'clock, and still the three of us waited—in a room with a TV we didn't watch, magazines we didn't read, and other people we didn't talk to. Hospital waiting rooms are no place for nice-to-meet-you small talk, especially when what you're waiting for is word from a neurosurgeon that your daughter is going to be OK.

Anne was in good hands, that much we knew. The surgeon, Dr. Sandeep Kunwar, was the recognized expert in the specialized procedure that would remove the tumor that had been the source of the problems that had plagued Anne the past year, including blood pressure so high, nurses taking it routinely said, "Let's try this again, Sweetie. There must be some mistake."

Cushing's Syndrome's high levels of cortisol were the cause of that and more. In normal amounts, cortisol is a good thing; it helps the body respond to stress and change. Too much of the hormone, however, causes significant changes in every tissue, every organ. A body can't cope with all that cortisol. And if left untreated, Cushing's Syndrome is fatal.

With the removal of the tumor on her pituitary gland, a full recovery was expected. And we knew the success-rate of this surgery performed by this surgeon was high. Still, sitting in that waiting room, I couldn't help but worry. Why wasn't Anne awake yet?!

On the other side of the world, Sergeant Diaz had been concerned, too. I had promised him an e-mail as soon as we knew how things had gone. But there are times, and this was one of them, when all the e-mails in cyberworld can't compare with the sound of a sister's voice.

Signs at the hospital admissions desk instructed patients to turn off their phones, and that's what Anne had done. So the best Roman could do was to leave a voicemail message she'd hear after the surgery.

Around 3:30, we finally got word to go up to the post-op floor.

"The doctor will speak with you now," a nurse said.

Up on the 4th floor a dark-eyed man in sky-blue scrubs came heading down the hall in our direction. Guessing he was Anne's doctor, I watched his body language for clues as to what he might say. His gait was relaxed, almost ambling. His eyes smiled.

"Anne's family?" he asked, extending his hand.

The surgery had gone well, Dr. Kunwar assured us, though it was a bit more complicated than he'd anticipated. The blurry spot on the MRI that was thought to be the tumor, wasn't one after all, he explained. Turned out the real thing lay hidden deep within the pituitary itself. Locating it was tricky. Removing it, even trickier.

"But I'm confident we got it," Dr. Kunwar said. Soon after that conversation, my husband and I followed Erick into the recovery room. Around our daughter, monitors beeped and pulsed and flashed digital numbers that kept on changing. Her big blue-gray eyes blinked at us over the gauze dressing that covered her nose. Standing at the foot of her bed, we heard her groggy, "Hi."

A single syllable has never sounded sweeter nor meant more—with the possible exception, Anne might argue, of one she heard later that evening: the "Yo" that began the voicemail message from her brother.

TO BAGHDAD VIA BOOKS AND BERKELEY

A few weeks later I traveled up to the Bay Area again, this time to attend a two-week teaching seminar at the Pacific School of Religion in Berkeley. Back in January I'd registered for the session that started the last week in July, after reading the book *Writing Alone and with Others* by Pat Schneider.

I'd come across that paperback while browsing at a bookstore, and initially bought it for what it offered in terms of new ideas for the adult-education writing course in memoir I regularly teach through the local school district.

"For more than a quarter of a century," the book's back cover said, "Pat Schneider has helped writers find and liberate their true voices. She has taught all kinds—the award winning, the struggling, and those who have been silenced by poverty and hardship."

With the writing I'd been doing for several newspapers about the war and my family's experience of it, I'd begun thinking about the possibility of someday leading writing workshops for war veterans. Schneider's book led me to a website where I found a West Coast seminar in the teaching method she pioneered.

The Sunday afternoon I arrived in Berkeley, after a nine-hour drive up I-5, I headed straight for Stern Hall on the campus of the University of California, where I'd made arrangements to stay. The dorm, located just a few blocks from the site of the seminar, is open during the summer months to groups and individuals who aren't college students. Those two weeks, I'd share Stern Hall with a few of my classmates and several high school teams attending a soccer camp. With Anne and Erick's apartment in Mountain View an hour's drive from the campus, the choice to stay in the dorm was as practical as it was economical. And I convinced myself it would be kind of fun to experience dorm life again as a fiftysomething woman. Showers down the hall. Narrow beds. Cafeteria food.

"Just stay away from frat parties, Mom," Roman kidded when I'd told him of my back-to-school plan.

But the typical response from friends and family to my dorm idea ran more along the lines of, "Are you crazy?"

Maybe, a little. Especially in light of something I hadn't counted on: a record-breaking heat wave—the worst in fifty-seven years, the newspapers said—that made the temperature in my south-facing room soar into the 120-degree range, rivaling the heat of high noon in summertime Baghdad. The dorm didn't have any air-conditioning. In that part of the country, it's rarely needed. When things finally cooled down, more than 139 deaths in Northern California alone would be attributed to the week-long heat wave. There were moments in Stern Hall when I thought I might be one of them.

But the experience did give me a glimpse into the kind of conditions Roman had been living in for months—with this significant difference: From my room's open windows I could hear young people chatting, singing, and laughing in the courtyard below. Not sniper fire. Not mortar rounds.

But thoughts of the war were never far away.

On the wooden desk next to the bed I placed a few of the books I'd brought with me, including Robert Jay Lifton's *Home from the War: Learning from Vietnam Veterans*. With no TV, limited Internet access, and home five hundred miles to the south, I anticipated having more time than usual to read and to reflect.

While I was there, I spent several late nights with Mr. Lifton, a professor of psychiatry and psychology at the City University of New York, and with the combat veterans he'd come to know through the rap groups he led back in the early seventies.

Lifton addresses the massacre at My Lai in his book's early chapters. On March 16, 1968, a U.S. Army platoon led by 2nd Lt. William Calley, went into that village shooting, believing it was an enemy position. But after the first civilians were killed by errant gunfire, the soldiers, it was reported, began attacking every living thing—people, animals—with guns, grenades, and bayonets. One veteran who was there talks about the feeling of unreality, the feeling that "it really wasn't happening."[18] And the question arises: How *could* something like that happen?

Lifton makes no excuses for the murder of hundreds of unarmed Vietnamese civilians, mostly women and children, by those American forces, but he does shed light on circumstances that can lead to that kind of darkness.

Especially in a war involving an insurgency and without clear battle lines, the feeling of a lack of genuine purpose can easily take hold among soldiers, the feeling of "being adrift in an environment not only strange and hostile but offering no honorable encounter, no warrior grandeur."[19]

Lifton goes on to attribute to activist-philosopher Jean-Paul Sartre this description of an atrocity-producing situation: "a counterinsurgency war undertaken by an advanced industrial society against a revolutionary movement of an underdeveloped country, in which revolutionary guerrillas are inseparable from the population."[20]

It's not uncommon for a sense of absurdity and moral inversion to pervade an environment like that. Lifton calls such a place a "counterfeit universe," and in it the ethical sensitivity that impels a soldier against adjusting to evil comes under constant assault, internally and externally. The death of one's comrades at the hands of the enemy, for instance, can cause not only a profound sense of guilt in those who survive, but also a primal rage and with it, a lust for revenge.

Those who fight our wars—all kinds, not just insurgencies—become aware of "the disparity between romantic views of heroism expressed 'back home' and the reality of degradation and unspeakable suffering they have witnessed, experienced, and caused."[21]

Reading Lifton's book, I couldn't help sometimes but substitute the word "Iraq" for "Vietnam" in the text—for instance, in this section where he writes of the returning veterans' struggle to find some sort of meaning in what they have lived through:

> One can say that, with the *Iraq* War, a vast American potential for the counterfeit has become manifest. From the atrocity-producing situation in *Iraq*; to the military-political arrangements responsible for it; to the preexisting but war-exacerbated antagonisms around race, class, ethnicity, and age; to the war-linked economic recession; to collusion in the war's corruption by virtually all professions and occupations—what is there left we can call authentic? To ask that question is to assume that there *is* something left. But that something has to be sought out and re-created.[22]

That search for what is true—and with it, a coming-to-terms with the war and one's role in it—becomes for the combat vet the work of a lifetime. It is also, Lifton rightly maintains, a responsibility all of us, as Americans, must share in.

～

Now I pick up the red spiral notebook that was my daytime companion those weeks in Berkeley. On the brown cardboard of its back cover, I read the tips I jotted there about places to visit—Black Oak Books, Peet's Coffee on Vine and Walnut, Sol's Deli, the Cheeseboard Pizza Collective—compliments of some of the locals among the workshop's twenty-plus participants, an eclectic group of writers and editors, chaplains and teachers, youth leaders, social workers, and artists.

On the tablet's red cover is a sentence I don't remember writing, but the penmanship is mine: "Simply speaking your truth heals." I flip open the notebook and find page after page covered with my loopy schoolgirl script. Lecture notes. References to research studies. Ideas for exercises and writing prompts.

At the core of Schneider's method of teaching is the writing that participants do at each session in response to suggestions, called prompts, the workshop leader provides. After writing together for twenty minutes, the people in the workshop are invited to read aloud what they've written. The group listens and responds, offering feedback on what struck them as strong and compelling in the new writing they've just heard.

What sets this method apart from others that involve read-and-critique is Schneider's insistence that everything read aloud be treated as if it were fiction. When people in the group offer feedback, they refer to "the narrator," the teller of the story, not "you, the author." What this does is create the safety to write what is real and true. The group's focus is always on the writing itself, not on the life experiences of the writer. It's not a therapy session. It's a writing group. But the end-result is often therapeutic.

Schneider says in her book, "When we write, we create, and when we offer our creation to one another, we close the wound of loneliness and may participate in healing the broken world."[23] The task of a good writing teacher is to create an environment that allows that to happen. An environment of trust, where writers feel free to take risks—emotionally and intellectually, as well as stylistically.

In the seminar, we were given frequent opportunities to experience the method firsthand. Sharon Bray, the workshop leader, provided prompts at several of the sessions. We'd listen—sometimes, at her suggestion, with our eyes closed—and then we'd set to work, filling our notebooks with words and thoughts jump-started by a photo, an object, a poem, or a phrase as fundamental as "I remember."

The prompts were the paths, we discovered, that led to the topics we wanted to write about, or in some cases, needed to write about.

For me that week, all roads led to Roman.

Now my eyes fall near the top of the lined page where I printed the words "Basket/Object Exercise." I remember watching at that day's session as Sharon placed—one by one—some thirty random objects on a blanket she'd spread out on the floor in the middle of the room. A wooden spoon here, a Barbie doll there, a crumpled pack of cigarettes between them. Her placement of these things had the quality of ritual, like someone performing a Japanese tea ceremony. When she finished, she invited each of us to choose one of the objects, pick it up, take it back to our seats, and write whatever images or memories came to mind.

Bypassing a shaving brush and a set of old keys, I reached for a child's pajama-top with a Superman "S" emblazoned on the front. Between my thumb and forefinger, the faded fabric felt soft as a toddler's kiss. And with one small, dark-blue sleeve dangling from the writing surface of my seat, these words—more prayer than paragraph—poured from my pen:

He used to wear a pair of blue pajamas with the "S" on the front. When his hair was white blonde, when his eyes were bright and full of wonder—at every-thing living: curl-up bugs, bees, ants, lizards, crickets, his pet rat. Now he carries a machine gun in the "iyah" area of Iraq—Al-Mahmudiyah, Yusufiyah. And I wonder if, when he signed up and joined the Army, if some vision of himself as Superman drove that. Roman as larger than life, protecting us from terrorists, making the world "safe for democracy." If he bought the propaganda soldiers have to buy in order to do what soldiers do. He was such a skinny kid. Not into sports. Not a tough guy. The image of him as a trained killer flies in the face of all that I thought him to be. There's that word—"flies"—like Superman, "able to leap tall buildings in a single bound." What kind of superhuman qualities will he need when he comes back? How will he adjust? How will he return? Will he return? Return in the truest sense—to the core of goodness I know to be there. What kind of superhuman love will I need to have for him and for his wounded soul? I wish there was a magic cape—more than one—for everyone who needs one. A cape to throw over our weary shoulders and tie, loosely, around our ten-der throats where all those words we cannot say are caught. A cape that will lift us up—high above the hurt—where we can see each other against the backdrop of a clear, blue, limitless sky.

THE INNOCENT DAYS

AUGUST 2006

The bubbles danced in iridescent droves, but I wasn't sure where they're coming from. Nudged by the wind, they drifted out across the lawn over to the dozen-or-so kids tumbling in and out of the inflatable Big Jump set up there in the Burton's backyard. Then the breeze shifted, and the next batch floated toward the patio where the grown-ups sat, munching curly Cheetos, sipping Diet Coke.

I was one of them. So was Roman Sr. It was a Saturday afternoon, and we were there to help celebrate Ryan's seventh birthday. For the past three years, he and his mom, dad, and sister, Hannah, had been our next-door neighbors.

Another partygoer, Ryan's grandma, tipped me off about the bubbles. She pointed to a small machine perched on the patio cover overhead where every couple minutes it pumped out another batch. "Grandpa's idea," she said in a tone that indicated she wouldn't be a bit surprised if Grandpa were to get in line later to take a swat at the piñata.

I liked all the "kids" in the Burton's family, no matter what their ages. But Ryan, 7, and Hannah, 9, were my two favorites. In temperament, gender, and spacing, they were so much like the girl and boy who once upon a time had birthday parties in our backyard, it was almost spooky.

Hannah that summer was everything our daughter, Anne, was back when she was in the third grade. Dramatic. Artistic. Lover of all things pink and pretty. A little girl firm in her conviction that any outfit can be vastly improved with the simple addition of a tiara.

But it was Ryan who reminded me so much of Roman, it sometimes took my breath away.

Roman's second tour of duty would be over in a few weeks, and when it was, more than two years of his twenty-three would have been spent in a war zone.

Though we'd been able to hear from him only occasionally, I saw him everywhere—in school boys lugging their backpacks on Black Mountain Road, in teenagers joking around at Jack in the Box or skateboarding in the cul-de-sac, but most of all, in the little boy next door.

With his shy smile and sun-blonde hair, Ryan resembled my son at age seven in ways that went far beyond their physical similarities. For starters, there was this fascination with all things creepy, crawly, and scaly. Bugs. Spiders. Lizards. Snakes. Ryan could also classify every dinosaur by whether it's a carnivore, herbivore, or omnivore—just like Roman used to. Ryan had his own theories, too, about the dinosaurs' extinction, and needless to say, had a soft spot for bedtime stories set in the Cretaceous Period.

Another similarity, a fundamental one, was brought home to me in a story Ryan's mom shared at the mailbox after his very first soccer game.

She and her husband had been cheering on their five-year-old and his team from the sidelines. And for a while, their little boy was in the thick of the action, chasing the ball with the rest of the pack. But that didn't last long.

"Wait a minute. Where's he going?! What's he *doing*?!!" Ryan's broad-shouldered dad wondered loudly, his eyes following his son, who had just veered off to a less trampled patch of the playing field. With both hands drawn up just below his chin, Ryan proceeded to curve his fingers into claws, bare his teeth, and change his pace to a menacing lumber. He was still in pursuit of *something,* but it was not the soccer ball.

"I, uh, think he's, uh, just being a T-Rex again, dear," Ryan's mom murmured.

That story reminded me so much of Roman years ago. His different-drummer mindset. His impossible-to-pigeon-hole soul. Boys will be boys, I thought, or sometimes dinosaurs, and maybe later, even soldiers.

Against the backdrop of the war and the bad news it daily brought, it was bittersweet to live next door to this seven-year-old reminder of The Way We Were. I'd often think about the choices made, the paths taken, in the years since Roman celebrated that same birthday. I wished it were possible to somehow catch and hold again the innocence that once was ours. To grasp, in more ways than one, what we had when we had it.

Back at the party, Ryan made a wish and blew out the candles on the chocolate cake his mom made. And the bubbles from the bubble machine continued their wobbly waltz. Swirling in the sunlight all around us, they shimmered briefly, and then—just like that—were no more.

Part Four:
THE JOURNEY
HOME BEGINS

THE SOLDIERS RETURN

SEPTEMBER 2006

The cavernous hangar on the airfield at Fort Campbell, Kentucky, echoed with the voices of families and friends, each waiting for a soldier—theirs—to return from a year in Iraq. In the bleachers along the side walls, hand-lettered posters told the story: "We love you, Daddy!" "My hero!" "We missed you!"

Roman Sr. and I sat in one of the top rows. We had flown in from San Diego that morning so we could say to our son in person, "Welcome home."

The crowd quieted a little in anticipation, then erupted in a roar of pure joy as the hangar's massive metal doors were slid open. There in the sunlight, some two hundred soldiers, moments ago on a North American 767 charter plane, stood together in formation as they had for many months, then marched inside.

"There he is! There's Roman!" my husband said, pointing to a tall young man in the second row. That soldier looked straight ahead at first, then turned his head to scan the crowd, spotted us waving, widened his eyes, and smiled, shyly it seemed.

But reunions would have to wait a while longer—for a speech and an invocation and, according to the program I was holding, two whole verses of "The Army Song."

When Roman looked up in our direction, I wondered if he also saw, as I did, all who were with him and us in spirit at that moment: His sister and her husband, who were back in Northern California. The relatives who'd sent him care packages of peanut butter and homemade cookies, mixed nuts, and funny DVDs. Neighbors who had added his name to prayer lists at their churches. Strangers who had come to know him through essays I'd written, and who'd e-mailed me to say, "Sergeant Diaz and the men of Bravo Company are in my thoughts and prayers." Friends who wept at the news last week that Roman was, at long last, coming home.

The ten soldiers from Roman's company who came home this past year in flag-draped boxes were among us, too, as were their wounded comrades, more than thirty, recovering in the States. Every heart in that hangar held the families and the far-flung communities of all those men. The actual head count totaled somewhere near 500, but thousands, hundreds of thousands, millions even, sat shoulder-to-shoulder in those bleachers.

My father, Roman's grandfather, was there beside me, even though he had been laid to rest in a veteran's cemetery eighteen years ago, when Roman was in kindergarten. In World War II, Dad landed on the beaches of Normandy, fought through to Paris, and at the war's end, saw—close-up—the horrors of the Holocaust in places like Bergen-Belsen. All he would ever say about those experiences was a rueful, "War is hell."

The men of Roman's platoon would surely agree.

At last the ceremony in the hangar ended, and my husband and I made our way down the bleacher stairs and into the crowd surging around the soldiers. At six-feet, two-inches, Roman was easier to track than most. We shuffled closer until the distance between us disappeared. And when it did, I threw my arms around him, and buried my mascara-streaked face into the front of his camouflage jacket.

"Roman," I breathed.

"Mom," he answered.

That was all.

That was everything.

～

In our hotel suite later, after a nice dinner at the best Mexican restaurant we could find in Clarksville, Tennessee, I took a gift-wrapped package out of my suitcase and over to the king-sized bed where Roman had stretched out. When his return from Iraq seemed imminent, I thought long and hard about a meaningful gift to mark a day like this one.

"This is for you," I said, sitting down beside him.

"Me?" he teased. He sat up, proceeded to unwrap the gift I'd just handed him, then looked at me with a puzzled expression.

"It's Grandpa's bathrobe," I told him. "After he died, Grandma asked if there was something of his I wanted to keep. I took this, and it's hung in my closet all these years. I remember my father wearing it at breakfast every morning when I was a girl. To me, it was always so him. And now, I want it to be yours."

After all that Roman and his comrades had been through, I was sure they would struggle, as soldiers have in the past, with how to come to terms with what they had experienced. Poet Archibald MacLeish, himself a veteran of World War I, spoke to this point in a memorial poem in which fallen soldiers say to the living, "Whether our lives and our deaths were for peace and a new hope or for nothing we cannot say; it is you who must say this. We leave you our deaths. Give them their meaning." This is the lifelong task that falls to those who come home from war. It is life's challenge to the rest of us, too.

Holding his grandpa's robe in one hand, Roman drew me closer with the other. His eyes softened, and he planted a kiss on the top of my head. "Thank you, Mom," he whispered. "Thank you."

THE ROAD HOME

OCTOBER 2006

For the two weeks Roman was here in San Diego, home on leave, a small gift-box sat untouched on a corner of the desk in his bedroom at the end of the hall. In it, a pewter ID bracelet engraved on one side with his initials, and on the other—the inside side—a favorite line from a poem by William Stafford that seemed appropriate, given where Roman had just been, and all that he'd lived through.

I have woven a parachute out of everything broken, my scars are my shield.[24]

I'd given the bracelet to Roman along with his grandfather's bathrobe the day he returned from Iraq. It was a small way, I thought, of acknowledging the hardships of this deployment: the deaths of his comrades, the encounter with an IED that earned him a Purple Heart, a deaf ear, and flecks of shrapnel embedded forever near his brown eyes. That chosen line was also meant to convey a belief in our human capacity to be as resilient as life can be hard.

In the hotel room that evening in Tennessee, still smiling over the plaid robe that rested beside him on the bed, Roman opened the box that held the bracelet. He took it out, turned it over in his hands, and read the inscription for the first time. He grew somber. Said nothing for several long seconds. Then he attempted to put it on and quickly pronounced it, "Too big."

"That's OK. I'll take it to a jeweler in San Diego and get a couple links taken off," I volunteered. "It'll be ready to wear when you come home!"

Soldiers returning from war are required to report in for a series of debriefing meetings on base their first weeks back on American soil. Official leave—and with it, trips to wherever home might be—is allowed only after this initial period of transition.

Roman shrugged in answer to my fix-it plan. "Yeah, sure, if you want to," he said. Then he dropped the bracelet into the tissue-lined box, shut the lid, and handed it back.

~

The re-sized ID was waiting for him when he arrived home a few weeks later to "Welcome Back" banners taped to the garage doors of neighbors up and down our street. They came to a big party at our house later that same day, along with friends of his from as far back as first grade. Godparents. Moms and dads from car pools years ago. The little kids next door with their crayon-drawn cards. The principal of his old middle school. The teenager who'd taken care of SpongeBob whenever my husband and I went out of town.

"You must be so glad he's back," they all said.

And I was. Though I was pretty sure the young man standing in the family room thanking everyone for coming was not the same one who joined the Army four years ago after high school. How could he be?

War inevitably transforms those in it, especially the ones who've faced combat. In the line of duty, they have seen and done and felt things the rest of us cannot know. Adjusting to peace can take some time. That's to be expected.

For the two weeks Roman was home, I watched this adjustment begin. Most of the time it seemed as if the past few years had never happened. But then there were other times, moments when a certain sadness would move across his face like a sudden summer storm.

He was much more willing to talk about his new ten-megapixel digital camera or the rock concert he'd been to the night before, than to say anything about the war. And I was careful not to ask. Yet the afternoon we took a walk around Lake Miramar, near the end of his leave, he was the one who pointed out the reedy shoreline's similarity to the terrain he and his men patrolled near the Euphrates.

"You know, it's just a matter of luck, that I'm here at all, that I'm even alive," he continued.

Then he opened up a bit about the men his platoon had lost. And I shared with him how, when he was deployed, I held my breath every time I drove onto our street, praying I wouldn't find an official-looking car waiting in front of the house. In the not-so-easy give-and-take of that conversation, the times when we both grew silent said more than words ever could.

In *Home from the War*, Robert Jay Lifton writes of the essential struggle soldiers go through to redefine who they are, when the battlefield's finally behind them. And an important part of that process lies in confronting that experience, claiming it, owning it, painful and complicated as it might be. It is the only way to move forward, Lifton says. As one Vietnam vet in the book puts it, "The more I refused to forget . . . the stronger I felt."[25]

～

On the day before he was due to fly back to Fort Campbell, Roman shuffled into my home office, fumbling with something near the base of his upturned hand.

"Hey, Mom, can you help me with this?" he asked casually.

I looked up from my computer screen, met his questioning eyes, then turned to help him fasten the tricky clasp of the ID bracelet that had been sitting in its box all this time.

"There you go," I said, as lightly as if I'd just put a Scooby-Doo Band-Aid on a skinned knee. But there was more going on there, and I think we both knew it. With the soft click of that clasp, I felt that even though early the next day he'd once again be leaving San Diego, my son had, in truth, taken his first step in the long trip home.

GUERNICA REVISITED

U.S. Deaths in Iraq in 2006: 791   Total since the war began: 2,962
Wounded in 2006: 6,580   Total since the war began: 22,565[26]

Estimates of war-related Iraqi fatalities since March of 2003 range from 55,000[27] to 655,000.[28]

JULY 2007—MADRID, SPAIN

No canvas, not even Picasso's, can hold all the anguish that is war. But if any painting can be said to come close, it is his *Guernica*. Eleven-feet six-inches tall, twenty-five-feet eight-inches wide, it hangs in a long, white-walled room on the second floor of Spain's Museum of Modern Art, the Reina Sofia in Madrid. And the reasons that had led me there included as many shades of gray as the work itself.

From the far side of the room Roman walked over to where I was standing. The rest of our little tour group—my husband, our daughter Anne and son-in-law Erick—had for the time being wandered off to other wings.

When Roman's time in the Army officially ended at Fort Campbell in January, I was sure then he'd come home to California for good. But he chose instead to stay in Kentucky for a while, renting a house with a buddy from his platoon in a small town near a peaceful lake, making do with his combat-pay savings, and working only at putting the war behind him. He played with his Xbox. Took up the guitar. Tinkered with his truck. Shared his room and sometimes his pillow with a puppy named Chester.

"Just chillin,'" he'd say when he'd call home occasionally.

For anyone who has ever loved a soldier returning from war, the worry doesn't end with the welcome-home hugs.

"Be patient. Give him time," my husband said. "I think he's doing what he needs to do right now." Those first months out of the service, Roman, it seemed, was still determined to be an "Army of One."

That's why I was surprised when he jumped at the chance to join the family on a much-anticipated ten-day vacation to Spain.

He had been to Spain once before—six years earlier, with his high-school art class the summer after he graduated. On that trip, he'd met "a cute girl" he liked a lot. Her name was Jesy Daghbas. She was on the same European tour with her art class, a group from a high school in the Los Angeles area. A visit to the Reina Sofia was part of their itinerary.

I remember how Roman talked about the first time they saw *Guernica*.

"Just being in the same room with that painting was . . . ," he paused, searching for the right words. If he had finished that sentence with something like "way cool," something flip and typical of the teenager he was back then, I probably wouldn't still remember that conversation. But the experience transcended that. Hearing him speak of it redefined for me forever what art appreciation is really all about. Henry McBride, the leading New York art critic in Picasso's day, couldn't have expressed it better. Just being in the same room with that artist's masterwork was, Roman said solemnly at age seventeen, "a *privilege.*"

～

With a museum cassette-player in one hand, I stood before that same huge canvas six years later, listening to a self-guided-tour recording. I already knew that Picasso created the painting in reaction to the Nazi's 1937 annihilation of Guernica, a small Basque village in northern Spain. Pounded by bombs for three hours in a just-for-practice show of force, the town burned for three days. Sixteen hundred civilians—men, women, and children—were killed or wounded. The aerial bombardment, unparalleled in military history at that time, had no specific military objective. It aimed instead to dramatically demoralize the population. Shock them. Awe them.

As I listened, Roman joined me in front of *Guernica*. His forearm came to rest casually upon my shoulder. I slid one arm around his waist and with my other hand, removed my earphones and offered him the cassette player. He shook his head.

There was nothing on that wall that he didn't know.

Facing *Guernica* together in the hushed, almost church-like atmosphere of that section of the museum, neither of us said anything. The painting said it all. Its fragmented images spoke not only of the violence and brutality suffered by one tiny town in Spain seven decades ago; they screamed of the inhumanity of war itself. And yet—and yet—from that, came this: the stark and heartrending beauty of the painting that has been called "modern art's most powerful antiwar statement."

That moment in Madrid had a full-circle feeling to it. Being in the same room with that monumental work, and being able to stand there beside my son, who at age twenty-three already knew enough of death to last a lifetime, moved this mother beyond words. To borrow one of Roman's: the *privilege,* that day, was mine.

Photo by Sue Diaz.

THE NOTEBOOKS

There isn't room in this brown box for much more, but it seems to me the spiral notebooks from the writing workshops I've been leading for war veterans belong in here as well. So I head down the hall to my office off the living room and carry back the small stack of them I've stored on the shelf near my reading chair.

The heart of each workshop session involves writing together. I offer a prompt—a word, a phrase, an object—to get pens moving. Then I push the button on my iPod player and with a Bach cantata or a George Winston piano solo playing softly in the background, the group writes for twenty minutes. So do I. At the end of that time, we take turns reading aloud the words we've just poured out on paper. In the spirit of shared vulnerability, I sometimes read what I've written, too. But not always. Some afternoons there simply isn't enough time, if all the veterans in the group are to get their turn.

Other days, my stream-of-consciousness ramblings feel too raw, too neurotic, or too motherly to share. On the days I take a pass on reading aloud, it's usually all three.

Many—too many, perhaps—of these notebook pages are filled with a parent's unresolved post-war angst. Here's one such entry, scribbled in response to the prompt: "Write about a song or songs that hold special meaning." On that Wednesday afternoon at the Vet Center, I wrote:

My first guitar, a cheap one, was black with a splotch of white plastic near its sound hole. I bought it back in the early sixties—the age of the Kingston Trio, Peter, Paul, and Mary; Pete Seeger.

What I liked about their songs—songs I taught myself to play—was the current of social change that coursed through the familiar chord progressions. And the idealism of the lyrics.

"The times they are a changin'."

"How many deaths will it take till we know that too many people have died?"

"The cruel war is raging, Johnny has to fight."

"When will we ever learn, when will we ever learn?"

And in spite of the somberness of those words, the message that came through was that maybe we would learn, could learn.

But now, forty-plus years later, the cruel war is still raging. And Roman had to fight.

Did the teenager strumming her black-and-white guitar have any idea that those songs would still be all too relevant when she reached her fifties? Did she ever imagine that one day her son would come back from the war with a deaf ear and a rattled brain and a sadness in his eyes as deep as any river?

"The river is wide, I cannot cross o'er. Neither have I the wings to fly. Give me a boat that shall carry two, and both shall row, my love and I."

I feel there is an expanse between us now—my son and I—that I cannot cross o'er. I look for answers. Listen for them with my heart. But try as I might, these days I do not hear them, blowin' in the wind.

I know Roman talks to a therapist at the VA, and I'm glad to hear that. Anne tells me he's shared with her and Erick some of the details of his worst days in Iraq. And that fact alone is good for a mother to know. But I know there is much I do not know. Much he hasn't talked about. And Roman seems determined to protect me still.

Putting the lid back on this brown box, I close my eyes for a moment and visualize him coming once again to sit beside me on the couch in the family room, like he did the day before he left for basic training. He lays his head on my shoulder. Again, I slip an arm around him and press my lips against his bristly hair. But this time, we don't sit together like that in silence as the shadows of a late afternoon grow longer. This time he hears me whisper, "I know the war is still with you. No doubt it always will be. But you're here. You're alive. You're loved. With all that—plus time, forgiveness, and the healing both bring—the war within, Son, will one day be won."

Epilogue

VET CENTER VETERAN
Spring 2008

"Those of you who'll be reading at the gallery on Saturday, we'll spend some time at the end of today's session rehearsing," I say to the seven veterans sitting around the long table in a small room at the San Diego Vet Center.

"Good!" Ernie nods, looking up from the spiral notebook he brings to this writing workshop every week. He's been in the program since it began several months ago. When one eight-week session ends, he signs on for the next. His seventy-page notebook, he tells me, is almost full.

This weekend, at an art gallery in the beach community where Ernie, retired now, lives and loves to surf, he and three others from the group will be reading in public some of the stories they've written in our Wednesday afternoons together.

"Hey, Ernie, gonna wear your wetsuit?" another member of the group—a veteran of Iraq—teases.

"Yeah, right," the silver-haired, Purple Heart Vietnam vet laughs.

In our time together, we've all gotten to know each other well. The group knows, among other things, that I have a son who served two tours of duty with the infantry in Iraq.

"How's he doin'?" one or the other of them will sometimes ask in the minutes before everyone arrives and the workshop begins.

They know that Roman returned to California at the end of last summer, moved in with his sister and her husband for a while, and began seeking treatment at the VA hospital for the kind of war wounds no one can see. They know he's been diagnosed with post-traumatic stress disorder—most of them can relate to that—and traumatic brain injury. According to a recent study by the RAND Corporation,[29] TBI has affected an estimated 320,000 soldiers who have served in Iraq or Afghanistan—some severely, and others, like Roman, moderately. In his case, TBI translates to day-to-day difficulties with memory, direction, and concentration.

The writing group was delighted to hear that Roman's recently become engaged to a lovely young woman named Jesy Daghbas. (They're living together now in the LA area. When the two of them were at our extended-family gathering at Christmas, I was touched to see how Jesy would always make sure she was on the side of Roman's good ear, so she could fill him in on bits of conversation he might have otherwise missed.) With her in his corner, Roman recently picked up a part-time job at Starbucks and has started exploring a number of options for the next chapter in his young life. He's been looking into art classes at a nearby college.

Like other brain-injured vets of this war, he received a Global Positioning System, compliments of Uncle Sam, to help him navigate the roads and freeways between Point A and Point B. I sometimes wonder if he ever thinks, "If only the voice on this thing that tells me to 'Turn right at the next intersection,' if only that voice could be as specific when it comes to Life's Larger Questions, like 'Where do I go from here?'"

Roman seems to be doing well, all things considered. But I'm learning from these veterans that the road back from war can be long, circuitous, filled with hairpin turns and huge potholes. The trip, in fact, can take decades. For some, it never ends.

I called and invited Roman and Jesy to Saturday's event. The gallery is about an hour-and-a-half drive from their Lawndale apartment. I thought it might be good for him to hear these stories, to see that telling them is possible.

"You two free on Saturday?" I asked.

"I think so. What's up, Mom?"

I filled in the details: veterans, workshop, war stories.

I heard him hesitating.

"Uh, yeah. Sure. I, uh, I think we can come," he said. "I'll, uh, get back to you on that."

~

My group's participation in the gallery's new-exhibit opening is being coordinated by the Kenneth A. Picerne Foundation, underwriters of this writing workshop and several other community outreach programs, most of them focusing on the visual arts. The work of those groups, ranging from paintings by at-risk youth to fabric art by low-income seniors, will be displayed on the gallery walls. My group of Vet Center writers will take the microphone at Saturday's opening reception.

Among the four who've volunteered to read, the level of writing experience varies. There's Dennis, whose writing of personal stories has been pretty much limited up until now to VA questionnaires for a PTSD claim. Sheri, who kept a daily journal while serving as trauma-unit chaplain in Iraq. Virgil, who's been working on a memoir about his experiences as the skipper of a Swift Boat on the Mekong Delta. And Ernie, a natural when it comes to writing, who on more than one occasion has cracked open our hearts with his truth.

He's been trying to decide which story he'll read, and has narrowed it down to two. The one he calls "The Dichotomy" is the story of a young combat vet's first day back from the war. It opens with a question, as blunt as it is brutal, that the soldier is asked within the first twenty minutes he is home: "Did you kill anybody?"

"No, hell no," the young vet says.

The questioner, a woman, counters, "Then why didn't we hear from you?! We thought something had happened to you. We thought you were in danger. We thought you were dead!"

Ernie writes, "I kept looking straight ahead not knowing what to say, I had been in danger; I was in danger every day. And though I had not died, there was death, there was death everywhere. It was a war, for Christ's sake. I had killed. I'd earned the right to be christened as a combatant, but I couldn't admit to it. I was afraid that I'd be banished and that people would be repulsed by me."

"You've changed," the woman tells him.

The narrator in the story grows reflective. "I had forgotten what I was like as a civilian. Had I really been talkative, animated, funny? I remember that I had been, but somewhere along the way I lost my sense of humor and then I lost my compassion. Not only for the enemy, but for myself. I wanted to survive, but in order to do it, I ceased to care about life. That was the dichotomy."

Later in the story the woman asks the soldier if he's up for the big Welcome Home party that's waiting for him.

"Yeah, for sure," he says.

But in the next and final paragraph, the veteran confesses: "I wasn't. I was worn out. I wished that I could sleep for a year, but the adrenaline rushing through my veins wouldn't let me. The metamorphosis of teenager to warrior was exhausting. I wasn't an innocent kid anymore, I felt much older than my twenty-one years. I just kept thinking, please, not too many questions. Please, just allow this tired old man to come home."

Ernie tells me he's leaning toward reading his "Silver Bullet" story on Saturday. Over the past few weeks, he's been working on revising and polishing it—or as he put it, "spanking it up."

I think it's a good choice. I know it's a brave one.

Before each of the four has the opportunity to do a read-through, I share with that group—unaccustomed as some of them are to public speaking—a few tips I hope will be helpful on Saturday: Take your time. Underline words you want to emphasize. Practice aloud at home. Try to make eye-contact now and then with the audience.

Ernie is the last to read. He walks over to the spot by the tattered couch where we've been pretending a microphone stands. He plants his sandaled feet. Squares his shoulders. Clutching the edges of two sheets of typing paper in both hands, he looks up and scans an imagined crowd. I follow his gaze—and envision a vast army of war vets, young and old, listening, side by side, with all who love them.

The old soldier clears his throat and begins:

For twenty-five years, the combat veteran had lived with all of the symptoms of post-traumatic stress. He had fought in Vietnam in the year 1968, but rarely, if ever, did he speak of the war. All of these memories had been neatly boxed up and compartmentalized, into a safe little area in the back of his mind. But as the years progressed, the box began to deteriorate and the recollections that he harbored began to seep through the facade. The dimly lit essence that had flickered in his soul, was surrendering to the complexities of life. The feelings of guilt, anger and depression became overwhelming. He awoke each morning with a sense of dread and despair. His flashbacks of the war ruled the night and soon began to follow him through the day, like a pack of hungry wolves stalking its prey. The physical wounds he received in battle had healed, but the emotional scarring continued to fester. It felt as if the flame that drove his spirit was being slowly extinguished.

He grew desperate, but was unwilling to surrender. He needed help, though he believed that no one, save another combat veteran, could understand his pain. He reluctantly and with ominous feelings of guilt and shame, began meeting with a therapist. During the sessions he blamed his depression and anger on his wife, his family, his boss, his job, but not once did he mention Vietnam. Then one day, he spoke of an ambush, a firefight that took the lives of the two men on either side of him. He recalled listening to the screams as he stood there unscathed. There had been firefights before, but nothing this terrifying. He felt like running, but there was nowhere to go. He remembered diving into the thick jungle carpet and firing his machine gun. The explosive outbursts of hand grenades and rockets jarred his body. His bones ached with the force of each impact. He could feel the heat of the enemy's barrage of bullets as the projectiles danced around him. The sweet smell of spent gunpowder permeated the jungle's lush, impassable surroundings. The hum of the bullets whizzing past was bizarre and unnatural, like the noise a horse fly would make, if it traveled at the speed of light. He heard the order to regroup and to move out of the kill zone. In his haste he grabbed the barrel of his machine gun. It was nearly white hot from the firing, but he couldn't drop the weapon. He felt the searing of his hand go all the way up his arm. As he spoke to his therapist, he began to cry.

He couldn't understand why he had made it home alive, when so many of his brothers did not. They were all great warriors.

"Then honor their greatness," his therapist replied. "Be the best man that you can be, the best father, the best son and friend. You need to fire one more bullet," she said.

"What's that?" he asked.

"Forgiveness, you need to forgive yourself. You made it home and it's okay."

So he fired one last shot, a silver bullet, and he understood. He couldn't save anyone then, but he could save himself now.

When he left her office, he felt as if a tremendous weight had been lifted from his heart. Something had ended or maybe just begun. It was an amazing feeling, both uplifting and calming at the same time. It was like the end of a storm, when the rain stops and the heavens open to sunshine and blue skies. The old soldier closed his eyes and felt the warmth of his spirit ignite. He looked up at the heavens and acknowledged his fallen brethren with a loving smile. He felt alive for the first time in many years and he knew that his life had changed. He had forgiven himself for surviving, and it was okay.

～

Saturday morning, the day of the reading.

The phone rings. It's Roman.

"Hi, Mom. Just calling to let you know I won't be able to make it to that thing this afternoon. Sorry. But we'll be down on Sunday. See you then, OK?"

I'm disappointed, but not surprised. War, it seems, is a place he's not ready to revisit. Not now. And not with me. There are battles he has yet to fight, bullets he has yet to fire. And these things, I now know, take time. His box is still watertight.

"Tomorrow? Sure," I say, trusting our "old soldier" knows that for him we will always be here.

Afterword
On Reading *Black Hearts*

I am sure I was one of the first to read Jim Frederick's book *Black Hearts: One Platoon's Descent into Madness in Iraq's Triangle of Death*, which was published in February 2010.

I had known it was in the works. Roman had told us several months earlier that he'd agreed to be interviewed by "a guy from *Time* magazine who's writing a book about my platoon."

"Well, just be careful," I advised him then, not knowing Jim Frederick nor his motives for delving into the awful events that surrounded Bravo Company's First Platoon in the spring and summer of 2006. Would this book he was writing, I wondered, end up being nothing more than a sensationalized account that capitalized on the horrors of that deployment? An exposé of soldiers gone bad? A work from which all the men in that ill-starred unit would emerge tainted by association and wounded even more in the re-telling? Truth isn't every author's reason for writing, and given the seriousness of what went down in Yusufiyah, caution in talking to a reporter seemed a good idea.

Roman talked to Frederick, as did many of the soldiers he served with, and then we waited. Finally, *Black Hearts* was released. A couple of days later, my daughter Anne called from San Francisco.

"Did you read it?" she asked.

"I finished it yesterday," I told her.

"You read it? Really? The whole thing? Mom, how could you do that?"

"Anne, how could I *not*?"

Black Hearts is not an easy book to read, especially for a parent of a soldier in that platoon, but it is a truthful one. Factual and fair. In seeking to understand how the atrocities committed upon and by some of the soldiers in the First Platoon could have happened, Frederick goes where the story takes him, to all those places Roman never wrote home about: lonely outposts, insurgent safe-houses, cold canals, farm fields crisscrossed by enemy fire, and streets as dangerous as they were dusty.

"During their year-long deployment," Frederick writes, "soldiers from the battalion either found or were hit by nearly nine hundred roadside IEDs. They were shelled or mortared almost every day and took fire from rifles, machine guns, or rocket-propelled grenades (RPGs) nearly every other day."[30] Time after time, the company commander's pleas for more troops fell on deaf ears. In the end, nearly 20 percent of First Platoon's soldiers lost their lives in Iraq.

This is not to say that unrelenting hardships and high casualties are any justification for the actions of the four soldiers—Spc. James Barker, Spc. Paul Cortez, Pfc. Jesse Spielman, and Pfc. Stephen Green—who would later be convicted of the rape and murder of Abeer Qassim Hamzah Rashid al-Janabi, a fourteen-year-old Iraqi girl, and the brutal murder of her family. Frederick in no way exonerates those men of their crimes. What he does do—in heart-rending, painstaking detail—is recount the myriad factors, including the breakdown in leadership, that gave rise to the conditions that made a "descent into madness" possible. In the last analysis, responsibility, Frederick rightly maintains, lies with each individual. But *Black Hearts* also makes the case that accountability can—and in this instance does—stretch up the chain of command.

For nearly a year, Roman lived in the crucible of that combat zone. And in reading *Black Hearts*, for a time, finally, so did I. It was so hard.

I know now that Roman should have died on December 22, 2005. He and three other soldiers were on a patrol that day when an IED, powerful enough to be heard ten miles away, exploded beneath their feet. Two of his comrades were killed instantly, but Roman and another soldier, Sgt. Tony Yribe, lived to fight another day. "The bomb was so big," writes Frederick, "that all four of them should have been dead."[31]

Just another day in Yusufiyah.

In a later chapter, Frederick put me with Roman's team in the middle of a vicious firefight. After one of their men was wounded, a lull in the shooting allowed that soldier to be medevaced. But there was still an insurgent in the house where the bullets had been coming from. Not sure if that guy was dead or alive, they called in an air strike to finish the job. But the pilot of the Apache helicopter was uncertain which house it was. A volunteer would be needed from the group on the ground to place an infrared signaling device, a locator about the size of a baseball, near the house with the shooter. Whoever volunteered would have to run—in the open—some 100 yards toward the house, an easy target for a waiting insurgent.

"Fuck it. I'll do it," Roman said.[32]

And I couldn't help but stare at the words and whisper, "No! Please. Don't!"

But Roman did, dashing out and going the distance to lob the locator near the house. It accidentally bounced into the front seat of a parked car. He ran back to his comrades, out of breath, only to discover that the device couldn't be tracked, its signal apparently blocked by the car's roof. Frederick tells me, "Diaz shook his head, swore, rousted himself, sprinted back out, all the way to the car, where he reached inside, pulled out the strobe, and put it on the top of the car; then hauled back."[33]

The Apache attack did not go as hoped. And though it blew some sizable holes into the house, the structure remained essentially intact. Three in the team decided to breach the place. When one of them was hit, Roman and two others rushed forward to pull him out of the front yard.

Acts of extraordinary courage and brotherhood—and the book tells of many—co-exist on the pages of *Black Hearts* with that other, darker story. Because of Frederick's book, I now know the things my son never wanted me to know. In *Black Hearts*, it's all there—the horror and the heroism, the cruelty, the carnage, and the courage. Roman's "box," which contains everything a combat vet has seen and felt and heard and done in the line of duty, is still his burden. But because of *Black Hearts*, it's possible for those of us who weren't there to look inside it, to see everything, and to learn something new and awful and real about survival—Roman's and mine and ours.

"You did some really brave stuff, Roman," I said when we talked for the first time about Frederick's book, a couple weeks later on the phone.

"Yeah, I guess so."

"And, gosh, you went through a lot!"

"You're right, Mom. We did."

Conversation about that deployment doesn't come easy, even now. I still tend to tiptoe around the topic. And my son still typically responds with just a few words. But there is real eloquence, not so much in what he says now, but rather in what he did back then. Reading *Black Hearts*, my eyes many times filled with tears; my heart, with a deepened appreciation of the human spirit and what it is able to endure, overcome, and even triumph over. That is where this book of mine now ends and where the next chapter in the lives of our returning warriors, and those of us who love them, begins.

Notes

Introduction

1. William P. Mahedy, *Out of the Night: The Spiritual Journey of Vietnam Vets* (Cleveland, OH: StressPress, 1986), 134.
2. Robert Jay Lifton, *Home from the War: Learning from Vietnam Veterans*, 389. Copyright © 1973, 1985, 1992 by Robert Jay Lifton. Reprinted by permission of Beacon Press, Boston.
3. Peter Marin, "Living in Moral Pain," *Psychology Today* 15, no. 11 (November 1981).

To Basic Training and Beyond—with SpongeBob

4. "October 2002." Infoplease. © 2000–2007 Pearson Education, publishing as Infoplease. 04 Jun. 2010 <http://www.infoplease.com/ipa/A0900849.html>.

War

5. "February 2003." Infoplease. © 2000–2007 Pearson Education, publishing as Infoplease. 04 Jun. 2010 <http://www.infoplease.com/ipa/A0906961.html>.

Seven Ducklings

6. "April 2003." Infoplease. © 2000–2007 Pearson Education, publishing as Infoplease. 04 Jun. 2010 <http://www.infoplease.com/ipa/A0906968.html>.

Answering the Call

7. "May 2003." Infoplease. © 2000–2007 Pearson Education, publishing as Infoplease. 04 Jun. 2010 <http://www.infoplease.com/ipa/A0906972.html>.

Grocery Shopping with Lucinda

8. "June 2003." Infoplease. © 2000–2007 Pearson Education, publishing as Infoplease. 04 Jun. 2010 <http://www.infoplease.com/ipa/A0906976.html>.

A Rare Snail-Mail Letter from Roman

9. "July 2003." Infoplease. © 2000–2007 Pearson Education, publishing as Infoplease. 04 Jun. 2010 <http://www.infoplease.com/ipa/A0906980.html>.

Weapons of Mass Illusion

10. "U.S. Casualties in Iraq," *GlobalSecurity.org*, http://www.globalsecurity.org/military/ops/iraq_casualties.htm (accessed June 3, 2010).

Not So Fast

11. "March 2004." Infoplease. © 2000–2007 Pearson Education, publishing as Infoplease. 04 Jun. 2010 <http://www.infoplease.com/ipa/A0920854.html>.

Coming Home

12. "June 2004." Infoplease. © 2000–2007 Pearson Education, publishing as Infoplease. 04 Jun. 2010 <http://www.infoplease.com/ipa/A0922008.html>.

A New Assignment, Another Trip Home

13. "U.S. Casualties in Iraq," *GlobalSecurity.org*, http://www.globalsecurity.org/military/ops/iraq_casualties.htm (accessed June 3, 2010).

Coming Home Once More to Say Good-bye Again

14. "June 2005." Infoplease. © 2000–2007 Pearson Education, publishing as Infoplease. 04 Jun. 2010 <http://www.infoplease.com/ipa/A0923153.html>.

A Soldier's Silence

15. "U.S. Casualties in Iraq," *GlobalSecurity.org*, http://www.globalsecurity.org/military/ops/iraq_casualties.htm (accessed June 3, 2010).

War As It Happens

16. John Crawford, *The Last True Story I'll Ever Tell: An Accidental Soldier's Account of the War in Iraq* (New York: Riverhead Books, 2005), 140–146.

Up in Smoke

17. Associated Press and Reuters, "Chronology of events at Haditha," *Seattle Times*, June 2, 2006, http://seattletimes.nwsource.com/html/nation-world/2003034321_hadithatime02.html.

To Baghdad via Books and Berkeley

18. Lifton, *Home from the War*, 37.
19. Ibid., 38.
20. Ibid., 41.
21. Ibid., 38.
22. Ibid., 187.
23. Pat Schneider, *Writing Alone and with Others* (New York: Oxford University Press, 2003), xix.

The Road Home

24. William Stafford, "Any Time," in *The Darkness Around Us Is Deep: Selected Poems of William Stafford*, ed. Robert Bly (New York: Harper Perennial, 1993), 10.
25. Lifton, *Home from the War*, 286.

Guernica Revisited

26. "U.S. Casualties in Iraq," *GlobalSecurity.org*, http://www.globalsecurity.org/military/ops/iraq_casualties.htm (accessed June 3, 2010).

27. "Fact Sheet: Iraqi War." Infoplease. © 2000–2007 Pearson Education, publishing as Infoplease. 04 Jun. 2010 <http://www.infoplease.com/ipa/A0908900.html>.

28. Gilbert Burnham, Shannon Doocy, Elizabeth Dzeng, Riyadh Lafta, and Les Roberts, "The Human Cost of the War in Iraq: A Mortality Study, 2002–2006" (study, Bloomberg School of Public Health, Johns Hopkins

University, Baltimore, MD, 2006), http://web.mit.edu/humancostiraq/reports/human-cost-war-101106.pdf.

Epilogue

29. Terri Tanielian, *Invisible Wounds of War: Psychological and Cognitive Injuries, Their Consequences, and Services to Assist Recovery* (Santa Monica, CA: RAND Corporation, 2008).

Afterword

30. Jim Frederick, *Black Hearts: One Platoon's Descent into Madness in Iraq's Triangle of Death* (New York: Harmony, 2010), xvi.
31. Ibid., 164.
32. Ibid., 216.
33. Ibid.

Bibliography

Crawford, John. *The Last True Story I'll Ever Tell: An Accidental Soldier's Account of the War in Iraq.* New York: Riverhead Books, 2005.

Frederick, Jim. *Black Hearts: One Platoon's Descent into Madness in Iraq's Triangle of Death.* New York: Harmony, 2010.

Lifton, Robert Jay. *Home from the War: Learning from Vietnam Veterans.* Boston: Beacon Press, 1992.

Mahedy, William P. *Out of the Night: The Spiritual Journey of Vietnam Vets.* Cleveland, OH: StressPress, 1986.

Marin, Peter. "Living in Moral Pain." *Psychology Today* 15, no. 11 (November 1981).

Schneider, Pat. *Writing Alone and with Others.* New York: Oxford University Press, 2003.

Stafford, William. *The Darkness Around Us Is Deep: Selected Poems of William Stafford.* Edited by Robert Bly. New York: Harper Perennial, 1993.

Tanielian, Terri. *Invisible Wounds of War: Psychological and Cognitive Injuries, Their Consequences, and Services to Assist Recovery.* Santa Monica, CA: RAND Corporation, 2008.

Parts of this book have originally appeared in the *Christian Science Monitor, San Diego Union-Tribune, Newsweek, Child Magazine,* and *Family Circle.* Reprinted by permission.

About the Author

Sue Diaz is an award-winning journalist whose work has appeared in such national publications as the *Christian Science Monitor, Newsweek, Reader's Digest, Family Circle, Woman's Day,* and the *San Diego Union-Tribune,* and whose commentaries have aired frequently on National Public Radio. A believer in the power of stories to heal, Sue has been leading writing workshops for war veterans at the San Diego Vet Center since 2007. The website she created—www.warriorswall.com—provides a place for veterans from across the country to write and share their stories.